Rhythms
of Grace

The Bible Reading Fellowship
15 The Chambers, Vineyard
Abingdon OX14 3FE
brf.org.uk

The Bible Reading Fellowship (BRF) is a Registered Charity (233280)

ISBN 978 1 84101 842 3

Rhythms of Grace is a revised and expanded edition of the Kingsway version
published in 2004.
This edition first published 2012
Reprinted 2012, 2013, 2014, 2015, 2018
10 9 8 7 6 5
All rights reserved

Acknowledgements
Unless otherwise stated, scripture quotations are taken from The Holy Bible,
New International Version, copyright © 1973, 1978, 1984 by Biblica, Inc. Used by
permission. All rights reserved worldwide.

Scripure quotations from *The Message* copyright © 1993, 1994, 1995 by Eugene
H. Peterson. Used by permission of NavPress. All rights reserved. Represented by
Tyndale House Publishers, Inc.

Scripture quotation marked NLT is taken from the Holy Bible, New Living Translation,
copyright © 1996. Used by permission of Tyndale House Publishers, Inc., Carol
Stream, Illinois 60188. All rights reserved.

Every effort has been made to trace and contact copyright owners for material used
in this resource. We apologise for any inadvertent omissions or errors, and would
ask those concerned to contact us so that full acknowledgement can be made in
the future.

A catalogue record for this book is available from the British Library

Printed and bound by CPI Group (UK) Ltd, Croydon CR0 4YY

Rhythms
of Grace

Finding intimacy with God in a busy life

Tony Horsfall

To Evelyn

You are a brave lady! Thanks for being with me and supporting me all these years, and always being willing to give me back to God.

Acknowledgements

My thanks to:

Alan Chew, who first had the vision and faith to publish *The Call to Intimacy* in Singapore.

Richard Herkes of Kingsway Communications, who had the insight to change it into *Rhythms of Grace* and make it more widely available.

Naomi Starkey, my editor at BRF, who has the confidence to believe it still has something to say.

Joyce Huggett, mentor and guide, and trailblazer in these things. I owe you and David so much.

Beverley Shepherd for 'The dream', such a challenging story and a fitting conclusion to this book.

For all those other writers who have inspired me, especially those quoted in these pages, and for permission from their publishers to use their work.

Recommendations

This is one of those books which has had a profound influence on my life. Tony not only reminds us of our need to slow down and simply 'be' with God, he also illustrates how we can do this, by providing practical guidelines on meditation and contemplative prayer. This book can enrich your walk with God.

Debbie Lovell-Hawker, Clinical Psychologist, Interhealth, London

I have read, and read, and read again this wise and gentle book, and each read has only increased my hunger to know and to love God and to walk the ancient pathways and embrace the age-old practices which Tony unwraps for us in its pages. This is a book for those of us who are weary of disappointing short-cuts to intimacy, and who long for a rich and deep and transformative relationship with God. In this book Tony reminds us of God's yearning for the love of our hearts, and shows us ways by which we can respond to that love. I cannot recommend it highly enough.

Mags Duggan, Redcliffe College, Gloucester

As a busy church leader, I find the invitation to experience the unforced rhythms of grace incredibly compelling. Yet to go beyond the invitation and actually walk in that intimate grace is another thing altogether. Tony Horsfall, a self-confessed activist, turns out to be perfect company for a busy Christian who wants to escape the destructive and depleting spiral of ever-increasing activity. Tony's book calls us to focus on the true Master of life – Jesus – who not only extends the invitation to this beautiful way of living, but has modelled it himself, and indeed offers to show us how on a daily basis. I hope this book finds its way into the hands of every active Christian, and in turn finds its way into their hearts and lives.

Erik Jespersen, Pastor, Woking Vineyard Church

Reading this book was like drinking refreshing water. It satisfied a thirsty soul. It pointed me back to Jesus and his releasing rhythms of life. Too quickly we are working for him rather than walking with him. I believe this is one of the most important books written in recent years because it is about depth and intimacy. For over-busy Christians and leaders, this book is a must. It is about much more than pace in the race. It is about going deeper with Jesus.

The Right Reverend Ken Clarke, Bishop of Kilmore, Elphin and Ardagh, Church of Ireland

The first edition of this book made me realise how hungry I was for God. I was a spiritual anorexic and I didn't even know how starved I was for something other than what I thought it meant to be a Christian. In England, at a retreat centre near Oxford, I absorbed the book walking fields, dangling hot feet in cold streams, sipping wine in pubs, and late at night huddled under warm blankets. Tony shares his experiences of becoming worn out following evangelical voices urging us to win the world for Christ and charismatic voices promising us to be able to do it faster and better. He found rest in the contemplative tradition. For the first time in many years I felt I could breathe and relax in God's company.

Fran Love, spiritual director and cross-cultural communicator, Arizona

By reading this book in a little church group, we learned to practise God's contemplation rather than to do more and more. Taking time to hear and admire our God is the key to our development. As we studied we experienced the nearness of God and his love.

Geneviève Utermann, Switzerland

Rhythms of Grace met the thirst of my heart and the longing of my spirit for guidance and direction in pursuing Christ's presence as opposed to continually trying to please him through performance. Instead of having to constantly work harder – the only response to salvation I'd previously understood – Tony helped me realise my desperate need to rest, reflect and spend time alone with Jesus. This book is water on a faith gone dry. May it refresh and renew your faith as it has mine.

Keith Dodson, Director of Human Resources, Missionary Maintenance Services Aviation, Ohio

Drawing on the insights and disciplines of contemplative spirituality, Tony writes without legalism to help us engage and encounter God through Christ in meaningful ways. This book will significantly widen our worship experience as we present our real selves to a real God.

Dave Bilbrough, international songwriter and worship leader

Written in a readable style, this book has been a helpful introduction for me to contemplative spirituality and its practice. I have been challenged to live by it, and to please God by my being with him rather than my being busy for him. I commend this book to all who desire to be drawn closer to God because he is pleased with who we are more than what we do.

Paul Tan, Overseas Missionary Fellowship, Singapore

Tony Horsfall would be satisfied if we could all say, 'I've got rhythm,' because he believes that rhythm is the secret to Christian happiness and fruitfulness. It is a rhythm of advance and retreat, going out and going in, activity and time with God. Tony gives down-to-earth guidance on how we build that rhythm into our lives. Seldom do writers make these great lessons so easily available to the average reader, but Tony does it. This is a wonderful book.

Major Peter Farthing, Salvation Army, Sydney

The words of Jesus

'Are you tired? Worn out? Burned out on religion?
Come to me. Get away with me and you'll recover your life.
I'll show you how to take a real rest.
Walk with me and work with me – watch how I do it.
Learn the unforced rhythms of grace.
I won't lay anything heavy or ill-fitting on you.
Keep company with me and you'll learn to live freely and lightly.'

MATTHEW 11:28–30 (*The Message*)

Contents

Foreword

> You've placed a hunger in my heart...
> You've caused a thirst that I cannot ignore;
> You've stirred a passion that will drive me
> into Your presence
> And I won't rest until You've heard
> My cry for more.[1]

That verse from one of Stuart Townend's worship songs describes so accurately the hunger that is gnawing at many hearts in these days when the pace of life seems to accelerate year by year. I have heard that heart-hunger being expressed in many parts of the world, from Singapore and Malaysia to England and North America. I heard it being expressed some years ago by the author of this book when he first came to our home to make a retreat towards the end of his sabbatical leave.

During that retreat and since, Tony Horsfall has tasted and seen for himself that 'the Lord is good'. Many readers and would-be contemplatives will be grateful to him for the time he has spent sharing with us some of the fruit of his own exploration into a form of prayer that has set him free to enjoy an ever-deepening intimacy with God.

The way the contents of the book have been spread out reminds me of an appetising buffet. Every chapter spreads before us a variety of tempting titbits. Sample them and they simply whet your appetite so that you find yourself going back for more – and more, and more. Take Chapter 8, for example. Here we read, 'If we seek him, we shall find him; if we have a longing for him, it will eventually be satisfied.' Such sentences are to be savoured and reflected on. As we reflect,

God's Spirit may well stir up in us a desire for more – more stillness, more sustenance, more of God's love, more of God himself.

The author makes this claim: 'When we meet God in the person of Jesus, we experience beauty – sheer loveliness, tenderness, compassion, charm and grace' (p. 68). That has been my experience as I have read and prayed with the contents of this book. That is why it is a joy for me to recommend the following pages to those who can no longer ignore or push away the passion for God's presence that has been planted in their hearts by God's Spirit. In particular, I warmly recommend it to those who find their hearts echoing the kind of sentiments that are voiced in Stuart Townend's song but who come from a church background that has never taught or understood the value of a more still approach to God.

As I have read, reread and prayed with each chapter of this book, there have been occasions when I have sensed the anointing of God's Spirit on the insights shared. My prayer as this little gem goes to print again is that through its pages and by the grace of God, readers will find themselves enriched and enlightened and that they will be nourished as they feast from the banquet spread before them. Whenever this happens, the author will be rewarded for the hard work he has poured into this book and God will be glorified. For this I pray.

Joyce Huggett

Introduction

'Don't stand still! Keep moving!'

I can still hear the sergeant-major-like voice of my Physical Education teacher booming across the playground. He loved to have us young boys running around on our toes, his own passion for physical fitness expressed in his fierce determination to develop our athletic prowess. No chance of dawdling while he was around! We learnt to keep moving, or else!

I guess that much of my adult life has been lived at a similar tempo. The world around us fears to stand still, and so do we. We are drawn into its motion, caught up in its activity, anxious lest we be left behind. Even as a Christian my life has been lived at pace. There has always been so much to be done, so many needs to be met, so many opportunities, and always so little time.

With these words I began my introduction to the first edition of *Rhythms of Grace*, published in 2004. The book began life in 2001 as *The Call to Intimacy*, published in Singapore by my good friend Alan Chew. I had just completed a short sabbatical from my work with the Equip missions training programme based at Bawtry Hall, a conference centre in the north of England. The book was the result of my exploration into contemplative spirituality. Coming from an evangelical and charismatic background, I had begun my search because of two key factors: firstly, an increasing desire within me to know God more deeply, and a sense of dissatisfaction with my own spiritual life; and secondly, a growing alarm at the number of highly qualified and gifted people involved in Christian ministry who experience burn-out. It seemed to me that contemplative spirituality, with its emphasis on realising our identity as God's beloved children and its focus on being rather than doing, had something significant to offer in showing us how to discover intimacy with God, and in making ministry more enjoyable and sustainable.

Invited to Singapore to teach on this theme of intimacy with God, I discovered a great hunger for the message of the book. The church there has grown rapidly in size and influence. It is dynamic and outward-looking, reaching out effectively in mission to its own people as well as to all corners of the world. It is also very driven, and highly demanding of its leaders and lay people. Not surprisingly, the invitation of Jesus to slow down and discover the rest he offers has resonated with many. I continue to visit regularly to lead retreats, conduct training seminars and mentor people in the rhythms of grace. It is a country I have come to love dearly.

In 2004 I was just starting out on a path that has changed my life. I wrote in the first edition, 'In my journey of faith, evangelicalism got me started, and the charismatic movement took me further. What I am feeling now is the need to journey on, to find the kind of spirituality that will take me deeper into God. The contemplative tradition seems to offer such a possibility. It provides what I call the third strand in the "rope" of an integrated approach to Christian spirituality.'

Well, I have journeyed on, both in my experience of contemplative spirituality and in my discipleship, following as closely as I can the leadership of Jesus in my life. Soon after my sabbatical, it became apparent that it was time to move on from Bawtry Hall and establish my own ministry (Charis Training), with a view to being more available to teach the insights in the book, and to lead retreats and Quiet Days for those taking their first steps in contemplative spirituality. I have been amazed at the opportunities that have opened up for me. I have also become involved in the pastoral care of missionaries and church leaders, both in the United Kingdom and overseas, and have had the opportunity over several years to put into practice in my own life the principles I teach to others. I would describe myself now as a 'contemplative activist'.

I am still on the move. I live a purpose-driven life (although I prefer the term 'purpose-led') and am still an achiever, but I think I am learning to pace myself better and to operate out of a place of rest. I am still an extravert, but I have discovered my introvert side and delight in silence and stillness and solitude. I am more secure in myself, too, knowing more deeply than ever that I am loved by God; I am finding my identity and worth increasingly in who I am in Christ. It's not that I don't wobble occasionally or sometimes allow myself to get overloaded and too busy, but integrating a contemplative strand into my evangelical and charismatic background has transformed me. I say that sincerely and without any exaggeration.

What has thrilled me just as much is the way I have seen others benefit from a similar integration. Stressed-out church leaders, overburdened mission partners, hardworking lay people – I have seen them all encouraged and uplifted as the truth of Christ's invitation to rest dawns on their weary souls. It has been such a privilege to lead so many on retreats and Quiet Days and to see the transforming work of the Spirit in the lives of those who are willing to slow down and encounter God afresh.

This is why I am so keen for *Rhythms of Grace* to be available again. My intended audience is the same as before, and my purpose remains unaltered. I have updated the 2004 edition and added a study guide so that churches and groups can learn to practise some of the spiritual disciplines I write about. Therefore the closing part of my original introduction seems just as appropriate now.

I am writing primarily for the many activists within the evangelical/charismatic section of the church. You may be a mission partner energetically serving God in a cross-cultural location. You could be a minister or pastor, busily seeking to build the church in a postmodern world. Or you might be one of that great legion of faithful church members, toiling away tirelessly at the heart of your local congregation. Whoever you are, I want to encourage you to open yourself up to new things, to explore and experiment with tried and tested ways of developing the spiritual life, some of which may be new to you. Above all, I want to encourage you to respond to the voice of the Spirit as he calls us to greater intimacy with God, and offers you a place of rest within his all-embracing love.

Nowhere is that call more clearly heard than in the words of Jesus in Matthew 11:28–30. Here the Saviour offers to take our burdens from us, to exchange our wearisome labour for his divine rest. Eugene Peterson's vibrant paraphrase in The Message (quoted at the beginning of this book) expresses exactly the radical nature of what is involved.

Those worn out by constant activity, burned out by the demands of legalistic religion, are invited to find true rest and recovery of life by coming to Jesus. As they enter into relationship with him, they discover that he is no overbearing taskmaster, but rather one who loves them unconditionally and without reservation. This experience of grace leads them to a place of rest and acceptance where it becomes natural to want to keep company with Jesus, and to develop a rhythm of life that makes it possible to remain in that love and to grow in intimacy with him. Thus they begin to learn how to live lightly and freely, and how to serve from a place of rest.

That means a whole new way of living – a way of following Jesus that sounds both attractive and attainable.

Come to me

The two great gospel words are 'come' and 'go', the one a word of invitation, the other of command. The first speaks of intimacy, and the second of activity. Both are important in the Christian life, but our coming to Jesus must always precede our going out from him. For many of us, there has been too much 'going' and not enough 'coming', resulting in lives that are spiritually impoverished and lacking in both depth and passion. At this time the Spirit is reminding us that the gracious invitation of Jesus to intimacy with himself remains his priority and is the foundation of everything else in the Christian life.

1

Invitation to intimacy

Everyone longs for intimacy.

Whether we are young or old, male or female, we have an inbuilt need to love and be loved. There is a longing deep within each of us to be known and accepted for who we are, without having to pretend to be what we are not. We yearn for the freedom to be completely ourselves and to know that we are loved, respected and appreciated for who we are. We need to be able to fail and yet feel safe and secure, knowing that our acceptance remains intact, our value undiminished, even when our performance falters. We want to know that someone has seen the worst in us and yet loves us just the same. We ache for the freedom and wholeness that true intimacy brings.

Not surprisingly, most of us expect to find intimacy in human relationships. We assume that through friendship or marriage, our need for closeness, for unconditional love and acceptance, will be satisfied. Reality, however, tells us a different story.

Of course, human friendships can be sweet and do bring a measure of that for which we are yearning. Marriage, too, brings us closer to the oneness we crave, but even at its best it can never quite deliver that for which our innermost being cries out. Indeed, it was never intended to, for this inbuilt longing for intimacy is a God-given need, created within each one of us to draw us to the Creator of our souls. This is the 'God-shaped vacuum' of which a number of Christians have written over the centuries, which exists within every man, woman and child. Only in relationship with God can our need for intimacy begin to be fully met. Only in the final communion of heaven will it be completely and totally satisfied.

Intimacy is ultimately a spiritual issue because only God can offer the unconditional love that allows us to be ourselves and know that we are accepted and valued as we are. It is expressed in 'grace', the unrestrained mercy of God flowing towards undeserving sinners. It means that God is the one who knows the worst about us and loves us just the same.

Our yearning for intimacy is an echo of Eden, for, there in the garden, Adam and Eve lived in unbroken fellowship with God day by day, until sin came into the world and spoiled everything. Having been born as descendants of Adam, we begin life out of fellowship with God. The reason Christ came into the world was to give himself as an offering for our sin and to reconcile us to the Father. When, by faith, we accept the benefits of his saving death, we are brought back into relationship with him. Friendship is restored and intimacy can begin.

Jesus invites us into this living relationship: that is why he says, 'Come to me.' The gospel invitation is a call to intimacy, to closeness, to oneness. This is what Jesus is offering to each of us. He presents us with an opportunity to get to know him, to walk with him and see, from close up, how he does things. We can learn from him by sharing personally in what he is doing – the most effective teaching method of all.

All this we can do without fear that he will take advantage of us or abuse us. Because he is full of grace and wants only what is best for us, he will never ask of us what we cannot deliver, but will always work with us to ensure that we can achieve what he has planned for us. He will not overwhelm us with the demands of legalistic religion. His call is to a relationship based on grace, grounded on his unconditional love for us and guaranteed by the unchanging nature of his character. We do not have to perform to gain or maintain his acceptance, because we are accepted already and for all time.

In such a relationship, we can find true rest, the freedom to be ourselves and the confidence to be at home in his presence.

Grace therefore leads us to intimacy, and intimacy is what the Christian life is all about. It is a love relationship, and we are called into friendship with the one who is the lover of our souls. Once we know that God is for us, that we have no need to fear him or dread his presence, we can approach him with confidence, and intimacy becomes wonderfully possible. As long as we are afraid of him, thinking him to be harsh and demanding, an unpredictable tyrant, we will want to keep our distance. As soon as we discover the depth and wonder of his love for us, we long to be with him, to know him more fully.

The understanding that the Christian life is essentially a love story is thoroughly biblical and totally transforming. God is the divine Lover, and we are his beloved, and the drama of redemption is the story of his relentless love, seeking us out. Of course he has plans and purposes for us, but they are the plans and purposes of a lover. Those who are one in heart inevitably share the same desires. Christian service, whether in terms of world mission, social involvement, environmental care or evangelism, is the inevitable outward expression of intimacy with a God whose love touches the whole world. It is not, however, the reason for the relationship. The relationship is, at heart, one of love; without that love, service becomes duty and obligation and is robbed of its passion and delight. If we forget this, our relationship with God will be nothing more than a business transaction, an employer–employee contract, when all the time God is looking for an explosive love affair.

Brent Curtis and John Eldridge captured the essence of this idea in their excellent book *The Sacred Romance*.[2] As the title suggests, the book's intention is to call the church back to the heart of God and the discovery of the passionate nature of his love for us, so that we can learn to live again the adventure of faith from our hearts. Too many of us live from the outer life of duty ('I ought to') instead of the inner life of desire ('I want to'), because we have substituted activity for intimacy. Although in every heart there is a longing for a 'sacred romance', most Christians have lost the life of their heart and, with it, their romance with God. Curtis and Eldridge write:

> For many of us, the waves of first love ebbed away in the whirlwind of Christian service and activity, and we began to lose the Romance. Our faith began to feel more like a series of problems that needed to be solved or principles that had to be mastered before we could finally enter into the abundant life promised us by Christ. We moved our spiritual life into the outer world of activity, and internally we drifted.[3]

Their analysis of the situation is an accurate one, and perhaps you can identify with it. We are too busy for love. Life in general is busy and the Christian life has become just as hectic, increasing the tempo at which most of us live and leaving little time to develop our relationship with God. Intimacy in any relationship needs time to develop; spiritual intimacy, the cultivation of our inner life, is exactly the same. Like a couple who drift apart because they never have quality time together, many of us are in danger of drifting away from the lover of our souls. We have no time to talk, no opportunity to enjoy each other.

Notice the irony of the situation. It is the 'whirlwind of Christian service and activity' that is the root of the problem. Somehow we have shifted the emphasis away from the inner life to the outer life, from being with God to being busy for him. It is a subtle and plausible trap, for many churches applaud busyness and hyper-activity as spiritual zeal. In their eagerness to achieve their goals and reach their growth targets, individuals can become expendable and spiritual depth regarded as a luxury. Extreme busyness becomes a mark of distinction, stress a badge of honour. As Tom Sine has noted, we are in danger of drowning in a sea of busyness.[4]

This was brought home to me when I was leading a seminar in Singapore for a group of church leaders. The topic was 'Staying spiritually fresh' and about 30 people had gathered together. I noticed one pastor, in the minutes before we began, animatedly talking into her mobile phone. She made no effort to relate to any of the other pastors there, but instead made one call after another for about ten minutes. Then, as soon as the seminar started, her head dropped to the table and she fell asleep. Feeling concern for her, I hoped to speak with her afterwards, but as soon as we finished she shot out of the room, dashing to her next appointment.

Clearly some people find a sense of self-worth in being busy, and even church leaders can derive their identity from their work rather than from Christ. To be busy is to feel important, but we can be busy doing the wrong things and miss the thing that is most strategic. 'We miss God's best,' says Sine, 'because we have little sense of how to find a direction and a rhythm for our lives that flows directly out of our faith.'[5]

This overemphasis on the outer life, which so characterises the contemporary church, means that we have few people who can help us understand and explore the inner life. Other Christian traditions have a history of spiritual direction and mentoring, but in the evangelical and charismatic context we have developed expertise in the more pragmatic expressions of our faith – such as how to build a bigger church, how to develop seeker-sensitive services, how to be more culturally relevant and so on. We are inclined to spend our time meditating on what form the church should take in a postmodern world or evaluating the latest 'fresh expression' of congregational life. These are important, but they often leave us little time for getting to know God more deeply. We may need, therefore, to look outside our own traditions if we are to learn about intimacy with God and become skilled at helping people develop their inner life.

What is encouraging, however, is the growing hunger in many people to be more at home in the inner life, to know how to abide in Christ and how to receive God's love for themselves. Soul care is increasingly on the agenda, as is the longing for intimacy. As Steve McVey says:

> There is an awakening amongst many believers today who are no longer satisfied with the hustle and bustle generally known as the Christian life. Call it the deeper life, the contemplative life, or whatever you will. By any name this quality of Christian life is conceived in divine intimacy and born in quiet moments spent between two lovers. Many Christians who are dissatisfied with the emptiness of the noise are hearing His gentle call to something deeper, richer.[6]

This is the divine invitation that Jesus makes when he says, 'Come to me.' He sees the need of his people even today. Many are tired. Large numbers are wearing out, burning out or, at best, living on the edge of exhaustion. His heart of compassion reaches out, for he knows that there is something better, something more. He longs to draw us to himself and surround us with his divine embrace. He longs to introduce us to the rhythms of his grace so that we can recover our lives.

Recovering life

The contemporary church stands in great need at the moment, probably without realising it. Evangelical and charismatic expressions of Christianity have certain strengths, but also some inherent weaknesses. At a time when spirituality is so popular, what is distinctive about 'evangelical' spirituality, and what are the characteristics of 'charismatic' spirituality? What are their strengths, and what are their weaknesses? And why is there so much activity and yet so little knowledge of God? What is it that drives so many Christians to be so very busy?

2

Tired and worn out?

'SAVED TO SERVE.' These were the words, in bold letters, painted on the banner that hung across the front of the church for all to see.

Standing just ahead of the banner, Pastor Evans was in full flow, challenging his congregation once again in his own inimitable style to a greater commitment and involvement in the church's programme. It was the first Sunday of the new church year and he felt it essential to rally the troops to greater endeavour.

Halfway towards the back of the building, Sue listened as attentively as she could, her head slightly bowed, her body a little tense. She had heard it all before, having been a church member most of her life. As far as she could make out, the key word in the pastor's address was the word 'more' – more time, more money, more meetings, more witnessing, more commitment…

Inwardly she groaned. How could she possibly do any more? Sue was one of the most active members in the church. Married to a husband with a busy and demanding job, she had two growing boys to care for and a part-time job of her own. She taught Sunday school, was on the leadership team and hardly ever missed a Sunday service or home group. What more could she give? Inside she felt tired and drained, even a little defeated.

As her mind began to drift, quite suddenly another thought came to her. 'More,' she mused. 'Yes, there must be more to the Christian life than this. Surely this is not what Jesus meant when he spoke about life in all its fullness. This can't be the abundant life, surely!'

Although she didn't realise it at the time, it was a seed thought sown in her mind by the Holy Spirit, a thought that would lead Sue on to an exciting spiritual adventure. From that moment she determined to rediscover the joy of knowing Jesus, even if it meant doing less in the church. Somehow she felt instinctively that she needed more time and space simply to be with Jesus, to find again her first love. A longing to know God more deeply began to well up within her. A spiritual hunger was growing again in her heart that demanded to be satisfied and surprised even herself. It was the start of something wonderfully new.

Sue is typical of many within the evangelical and charismatic sections of the church worldwide. Committed and involved, they have given their all to serving God but find themselves, like Sue, tired and weary, longing for something more. There seems to be something lacking in our spirituality, for the way many of us currently practise the Christian life leads us more to activity than to intimacy. As a result, many of us seem to endure our faith rather than enjoy it, for it brings us increasingly into the busyness of the outer life and less and less into the vitality of the inner life. Worn out by this constant demand for effort, we let go of our anchorage in the love of God and lose the joy of simply knowing Jesus. It all becomes too serious, too pressurised, too exhausting.

It is worth pausing for a moment to consider our own spirituality and how it is expressed. It could be that there is something inadequate in our basic understanding of how to live the Christian life. It is not my intention to be critical here but rather to examine the approach to Christian living that many of us have enthusiastically adopted, without realising that it may not provide us with the whole story.

'Christian spirituality' is based on the central teachings of Christianity and describes the way it is practised in everyday life. Essentially it is about how we care for our 'soul' or 'spirit' and the means by which we maintain and develop our relationship with God. David Gillett, in *Trust and Obey*, says that it has to do with 'how we articulate our relationship with God in Christ, and the particular practical ways which we find most helpful in developing this relationship from within the whole range of Christian tradition and experience'.[7]

The shape of our spirituality is influenced by many variables, such as our theology, denominational background and personality, and the historical setting in which we live.[8] This means that there are many 'types' of Christian spirituality. So it is that we speak of 'evangelical' spirituality or 'charismatic' spirituality or 'contemplative' spirituality. Each adjective gives us a clue to the particular style or form of Christianity that is being practised.

What, then, is evangelical spirituality? Some people may object to the idea that evangelicalism represents only one 'type' of spirituality, preferring to think that it represents a fully biblical approach to living the Christian life and is therefore innately superior to other traditions. However, most writers on Christian spirituality objectively see it as one important expression among several.

Although some like to identify evangelicalism with the Protestant Reformation of the 16th century, most date its emergence from the evangelical revival of the 18th century and the influence of people like Wesley and Whitefield. Evangelicalism is usually described as having four central features: the place of the Bible, the centrality of the cross, a stress on a personal conversion experience, and active service.[9]

Since evangelicals regard the Bible as the inspired and infallible word of God, it is not surprising that they place such a great emphasis on the scriptures and recognise them as the primary way in which he speaks to us. This shows itself in the primacy of expository preaching, the practice of daily Bible reading, the formation of Bible study groups and the custom of seeking to evaluate everything by whether it is 'biblical' or not.

Evangelicals emphasise the centrality of the cross as the means of salvation and the focus of devotion. A substitutionary view of the atonement is usually accepted (although this has been challenged by some in recent years), whereby Christ is said to have died in the place of the believer, and there is a subsequent challenge to live a life worthy of the one who died in our place: 'To be gripped by Calvary love and to be motivated by it is the very heartbeat of evangelical spirituality.'[10]

Personal conversion is the way into the kingdom of God, and is emphasised as opposed to 'nominalism' – that is, having only the external name of a Christian without any heart experience. Individuals must be 'born again' and have their own encounter with God. This experience of repentance from sin and of faith towards God is essential for salvation. It may be part of a process or experienced as a crisis in a decisive moment. 'Individualism', therefore, is a distinguishing mark of the evangelical approach to Christian living.

The emphasis on service and on evangelism and mission (sharing one's faith with others, including those of other cultures) follows naturally. A deep sense of obligation lies at the heart of evangelicalism, releasing a dynamic of energy to be involved in the cause of Christ. Evangelicals are people who are active for God, whose faith affects the way that they live.

David Gillett adds two other characteristics in his own helpful appraisal to those already mentioned. Firstly, he highlights the emphasis on assurance. Evangelicals believe it is possible to know with certainty that we are saved. This assurance affects the 'atmosphere of faith' in which we live, giving confidence in God's promises, boldness in prayer and the certainty of heaven and eternal life. Gillett also mentions the pursuit of holiness. For evangelicals, the goal of living is to become like Christ and to express that Christ-likeness in daily life. There are divergent views as to how this is to be achieved, but holiness of life is a common aim. Sometimes this has led to a confusion of holiness with respectability, and middle-class values with gospel norms. This approach can sometimes also become legalistic and moralistic.

What about charismatic spirituality? The modern charismatic movement in Britain became increasingly widespread in the late 1960s, as part of an associated renewal movement that affected most parts of the world. It is now generally accepted that, after an initial period of stormy opposition, the evangelical church largely welcomed renewal and embraced the charismatic emphasis. As Dave Tomlinson says in *The Post-Evangelical*, 'It is now clear that the whole centre ground of evangelicalism has become charismaticised.'[11]

Many of the theological and spiritual roots of the charismatic tradition are the same as those of evangelicalism, and, of course, many of those who embraced the new movement would have described themselves first and foremost as evangelicals. Charismatic spirituality therefore built on the spirituality we have already described, but added some new features and modified some of the old.

Charismatic spirituality is distinguished by lively praise and worship, a particular emphasis on the baptism in the Spirit, the use of spiritual gifts in the local congregation, 'power' evangelism and the reality of 'spiritual warfare'. In particular, the gift of speaking in tongues is valued, as well as prophecy, especially personal words from God on behalf of individuals.

Renewal brought a new emphasis on demonstrable and emotional expressions of love for Jesus and fellow believers. These expressions are sometimes parodied as being 'happy-clappy' and 'huggy-feely'. In association, there has been an explosion of new worship songs and a multiplication of worship bands and worship leaders.

The leadership in charismatic churches usually recognises particular ministry gifts, such as the calling to be apostles or prophets (mentioned in Ephesians 4:11), and sees these gifts as being operational in the church today. A healthy charismatic church will normally include apostolic 'covering' (to provide direction and vision) and prophetic 'input' (bringing a sense of what God is saying to the congregation in the present moment) to ensure that it has good foundations.

Although always present in Pentecostalism, the charismatic emphasis on 'power' evangelism was deepened by the ministry of John Wimber in particular, bringing the ministries of healing and deliverance and 'signs and wonders' back into prominence, using them as a means of bringing people to faith. Times of 'ministry', when individuals receive prayer for personal needs, are now common in many churches, and some groups are even taking a ministry of healing on to the streets.

A final noteworthy characteristic of charismatic spirituality is the emphasis on engaging in 'spiritual warfare', based on the victory of Christ on the cross over Satan and demonic powers, and his ascension to a place of rule at God's right hand. This has brought into prominence the ministry of intercession, prayer marches, identificational repentance (asking God's forgiveness for the sins of former generations, such as involvement in the slave trade) and 'spiritual mapping' (seeking to identify where demonic powers are noticeably at work in a locality).

So where are we now? Neither the evangelical stream nor the charismatic one is static but both are continually changing and developing. Within both, there has been a growing acceptance of the need to incorporate social action as a valid expression of the gospel, and a growing awareness of the need to apply Christian living to environmental issues and the care of the planet. Both streams are tending to become increasingly fragmented, too, as these different emphases develop and different approaches to thorny questions emerge (such as the ministry of women, the inspiration of the Bible and attitudes to homosexuality). The general descriptions above remain valid, however.

The blending of the evangelical emphasis and the charismatic approach has brought great good to the church worldwide. Ideally, the combination of an emphasis on the word of God (evangelical) and an emphasis on the Spirit of God (charismatic) should have created a balanced but powerful expression of the Christian faith.

However, certain weaknesses remain, and may even be exaggerated by this marriage of traditions. The first of these, in my opinion, is the increasing lack of a first-hand knowledge of God in the church today – by which I mean not the finding of God but the intimacy with God that makes a real adult relationship possible, natural and comfortable. The second is the increasing emphasis on the importance of activity over intimacy, a major flaw that seems almost written into the DNA of both streams.

For all its emphasis on helping people to discover a personal relationship with God, evangelicalism seems to bring people so far but no further. This is one of the reasons why increasing numbers feel frustrated within evangelical churches, and was highlighted by Dave Tomlinson in *The Post-Evangelical*.

In his book, Tomlinson described how he had met many people who shared the same feeling – 'the feeling that evangelicalism is supremely good at introducing people to faith in Christ, but distinctly unhelpful when it comes to the matter of progressing into a more "grown up" experience of faith'. A more 'grown-up' faith, for him, meant the freedom to question or to doubt, with fewer predigested opinions and categorical conclusions. Such openness is essential, Tomlinson believed, in a postmodern world.[12]

Interestingly enough, he saw the postmodern search for spirituality leading in a particular direction:

The post-evangelical impetus… is to search for this fresh sense of spirituality in the symbolic and contemplative traditions of the Church rather than in the New Age movement. Failing to find much evidence of these elements in evangelical spirituality, it is inevitable that post-evangelicals seek to find them in ancient Celtic Christianity, as well as in aspects of Catholicism and Eastern Orthodoxy.[13]

This is why the integration of some aspects of contemplative spirituality into evangelical church life may actually also enhance our evangelistic potential as well as increasing our ability to retain the attachment of those already there.

For many people, the charismatic movement offered fresh hope of a deepening relationship with God. Gillett suggests that it met the need for 'assurance', which was lacking in many second-generation evangelicals,[14] and he may be correct, for the gift of tongues (although not necessarily given to all) is a very tangible confirmation of God's presence. However, even charismatic experience can leave a person still hungry for God.

The widespread interest in the Toronto Blessing in the 1990s, followed by supernatural outpourings in Pensacola and Lakeland (Florida) in the following decade, bear witness to the spiritual hunger in the hearts of many charismatics, especially those in leadership. With pilgrim-like devotion, many hundreds visited these locations, seeking a deeper experience with God. This very fact alone would seem to testify to the inadequacy of some expressions of charismatic spirituality. Can we not find God where we are? Is it really necessary to travel thousands of miles, at great financial and environmental expense, to encounter him?

We have to acknowledge that we have failed to teach people how to find God for themselves. Charismatic spirituality has become increasingly centred on personalities and focused on the impartation of truth by a few to the passive majority. So we have a plethora of conferences, celebrations and teaching events, plus books and magazines, web pages and blogs, podcasts and downloads, live streaming of services on the internet, and endless cable and satellite TV channels. What all this does is to create a second-hand faith, whereby we think we have absorbed truth simply because we have heard it from someone else. It encourages a dependency culture among believers. Rather than seeking God for ourselves, we can tune in or switch on to our favourite preacher and be 'fed' yet again.

There is little need to seek God for ourselves because we can receive so much spiritual stimulation from others. As long as the worship is good and the teaching inspiring, we can be seduced into thinking that we are deepening our relationship with God. However, the growing gap that exists between belief and behaviour in the lives of many contemporary Christians should alert us to the fact that all may not be as well as it appears.

In 2004, the Willow Creek Community Church in Chicago, famous for its 'seeker-sensitive' approach and producing first-class materials for small groups, conducted a survey of its members to see what progress they were making. To the leaders' alarm, the survey revealed that many people were not changing significantly. Indeed, they were still struggling with addictions, inappropriate relationships and emotional issues, and were finding it hard to put God first in their lives. Even more disturbing was the fact that 25 per cent of the more established church members described themselves as 'stalled' in their relationship with God. To its credit, the church responded to the situation, recognising the need to help its members develop their inner lives for themselves and to develop mentoring relationships that would help them go deeper into Christ. You can read about the survey, and the response to it, at revealnow.com.

More encouragingly, there is a growing hunger among charismatics for intimacy with God. Many are instinctively looking for something deeper, something more substantial. Worship songs express a more reflective mood and leaders openly share their own longing to know God more deeply. Those with a prophetic instinct would see this as a hunger being created by the Spirit of God, calling the church back into a love-relationship with Jesus. The time seems to be right to rediscover some of the 'ancient paths' of the spiritual life.

How can contemplative spirituality help us? The contemplative tradition encourages us to find an intimate relationship with God through silence and reflection, taking its biblical basis from Psalm 46:10: 'Be still, and know that I am God' (NIV). The implications of this verse are clear: (1) we can know God, and (2) there are some things about God that cannot be known without stillness. It seems that the best way to get to know God closely is to be still before him and silent in his presence. In such a context, God will reveal himself to us more fully.

This tradition can teach us, among other things, how to still ourselves and how to value and use silence. It can help us to listen to God and show us how to take in his beauty and his glory. It is about 'being' rather than 'doing', about resting in God's love and allowing our service to flow out of that place of acceptance. It emphasises becoming rather than achieving, and the focus is on finding our identity as God's beloved children rather than through our success, even in ministry. It is about coming to Jesus and knowing what to do when we get to him.

Within the tradition of the wider church (mostly hidden from evangelicals and charismatics) are the writings and experience of generations of believers who have trodden this path before us. Their wisdom can enlighten us and guide our path even now, if we have the humility to listen and the hunger to search. They can show us how to develop rhythms of grace that fit the context of the 21st century.

I look back over my own Christian experience with deep thankfulness for the way God broke into my life. Although I was not from a Christian family, I was encouraged to attend Sunday school and came to a personal faith as a teenager. The experience was real and deep, and I wept for my sins and knew the joy of forgiveness through what Jesus had done for me on the cross. I was shown how to read the Bible (with the help of Bible reading notes), encouraged to pray and exhorted to share my newfound faith with others. Soon I desired to give my whole life to God and serve him 'full-time'.

I went to Bible college and entered the world of evangelicalism proper. There I was taught 'sound' doctrine and, just as importantly, what was considered 'acceptable' behaviour. It was a challenging and stretching experience but I gladly embraced the whole package. I met some students at college who clearly had a dimension to their Christian lives that I did not have. They spoke about being 'baptised in the Spirit' and I began to hunger for a similar experience. Eventually, I had a particular experience of being filled with the Spirit and received the gift of tongues. This was in the early days of the charismatic movement, and there was a sense of adventure and excitement about what was happening, even if it was controversial to some.

This experience of the Holy Spirit revolutionised my Christian life and made me more open to whatever God wanted me to do. During my last year at college, I felt an increasing burden for the Chinese people and, eventually, together with my wife Evelyn (another benefit of being at college!), went to the island of Borneo (East Malaysia) as a missionary. There followed eight exciting years of church planting in a beautiful country where God was powerfully at work.

We returned to Britain in 1983 with two children and an enriched experience of God. I became pastor of a charismatic church in the heart of the Yorkshire coalfield. In some ways it was more pagan than Borneo, but God was still at work and the church grew. In 1993, I moved into a training ministry, preparing and equipping others who were going to serve God overseas. I now work as a freelance trainer and have the privilege of leading groups in different parts of the world on retreats and Quiet Days.

During more than 30 years of 'full-time' Christian service, the centrality of the word of God and the need for the power of the Spirit have been fundamental to all I have done. I am so grateful for the spiritual nurture I received and for those who helped me on my spiritual journey. But the journey continues, and I am as excited now as I have ever been. The same hunger to know God more deeply burns in my heart. I still stand on the word of God and still depend upon the Spirit's power, but from both word and Spirit I seem to be hearing God's call to the kind of intimacy with himself that requires some of the disciplines and insights of the contemplative tradition: to be still, and to know God in the stillness.

I believe that this is far more than God's call to me alone. It is the call of God to many who are like me – evangelicals committedly serving God and charismatics enthusiastically seeking his kingdom. The longing for greater intimacy is growing, and the desire for the 'rest of God' is increasing. It is a thirst created by God himself, which he intends to satisfy. We have come so far, and we know that the road still stretches on ahead of us.

However, an obstacle stands in our path, preventing many of us from finding intimacy with God. What is it? It is the second great weakness inherent within the evangelical and charismatic streams: the busy activism that characterises us, which we wear as a badge of honour and which inhibits our desire to go deeper with God. To this issue we now turn our attention.

3

Burned out on religion?

Evangelicals are busy people. They are always doing something and delight in activity. They seem to value busyness and prize 'commitment'. Indeed, the highest compliment is to be described as an 'active' Christian. For evangelicals, genuine faith results in energetic service for God. A job advert in a national Christian magazine seems to sum it up:

> Active congregation requires an experienced, dynamic Christian on a part-time basis (20hrs per week) to consolidate the existing pastoral work, and to expand outreach into the community.

I didn't feel drawn to apply myself, and I rather pity the person who got the job! I somehow doubt whether 20 hours would be enough to satisfy the expectations of such an 'active' congregation, even if the job holder was 'experienced and dynamic'.

Evangelicals sometimes fail to realise that such an energetic spirituality is peculiar to their own tradition, and that other Christians do not always feel the same need to be busily serving God. What is it about evangelical spirituality that produces such activism?

First of all, evangelicals believe in a God who acts here and now. They stress his immanence and involvement in the world, rather than his transcendence and mystery. Therefore, they expect him to be active, and, if God is active, they too must be active. The logic is that if God is committed to action, those who want to be close to him will involve themselves in his plans and purposes. 'God is not simply to be imitated in his holiness, but in his activity,' says David Gillett.[15]

The call to service is consequently a prominent note in evangelicalism. As R.A. Torrey said, 'The working Christian is the happy Christian.'[16] The reason why some Christians don't 'backslide' is because they are too busy to do so! C.H. Spurgeon added to this insistence on activity by telling younger ministers, 'Kill yourselves with work, and then pray yourselves alive again.'[17] Thus a tradition of hard work and total involvement has been passed down from one generation of believers to another, with laziness seen as a deadly sin. D.L. Moody, another father of evangelicalism, is quoted as saying, 'Laziness belongs to the old creation, not the new. There is not a lazy hair in the head of a true Christian... We cannot work for God without love... but the moment the love of God is shed abroad in our hearts, my friends, we cannot help loving Him and working for Him.'[18]

The second string in the bow of evangelical activism is the moral obligation that flows from the cross. We have already noted the centrality of the cross and the emphasis on a substitutionary atonement. Linked with this is a constant appeal to the moral obligation of the cross. As Christ gave himself for us, so we are to give ourselves to him. Charles Wesley, in his hymn 'When I survey the wondrous cross', puts it like this: 'Love so amazing, so divine, demands my soul, my life, my all.'

A life of sacrificial service is regarded as the only proper response to the death of Christ on our behalf. This sense of obligation provides much of the inner dynamic for the activism that characterises so much of evangelical life. The legacy of forgiveness is a debt to love.

James Gordon, in *Evangelical Spirituality*, sums it up with these words:

> Spirituality is lived doctrine. For Evangelicals that means the cross is to be lived. The self-giving love of God in Christ, the 'grace unspeakable' of a crucified Lord, ignites within the heart

of the forgiven sinner such fires of love, gratitude and wonder, that the only sufficient response is a life of self-expenditure, the total surrender of mind, heart, and will.[19]

A third incentive to be up-and-doing comes from the desire to share the good news with others. Evangelicals feel a moral obligation to 'spread the word' and are therefore committed to evangelism and missionary endeavour. To some extent, this is what Gillett calls an 'assurance-generated dynamism', fuelled by the evangelical belief that we can be sure of our salvation, and so be in a position to persuade others. It is also fuelled by the belief that people without Christ are lost and going to hell, which some see as characterised by eternal torment. Although not stressed as much nowadays, this understanding has always given added urgency to Christian service as far as evangelicals are concerned.

For a long time, evangelicals were suspicious of social action, fearing a watering-down of the gospel message. Gradually, through the work of the Lausanne Movement (an occasional worldwide gathering of evangelical leaders begun in 1974), it became acceptable to marry the two strands. Nowadays, given the gap between many communities and the church, social involvement is seen as an essential bridge in reaching out to people, an almost obligatory part of the average church's agenda. So we have parent-and-toddler groups, pregnancy crisis agencies, drop-in centres, soup kitchens, homeless shelters, youth workers in the community and so on. Increasingly, churches are being encouraged to be involved in Fair Trade, to be aware of environmental issues and to become 'green' in the way they run their buildings. All of this is good, but it increases the workload of local congregations and their leaders, as well as their sense of duty and responsibility.

In this context, the call to 'full-time' service has been prominent, leading to the unconscious feeling that anyone who is serious about serving God will leave secular employment and involve themselves (usually for minimal financial reward!) in Christian work. The heroes and heroines of evangelicalism are those who have done just that – missionaries and church leaders, in particular. Those who have not felt such a call risk the temptation of feeling 'second-rate', and may want to show that they are as committed as others by working just as hard for God in their free time.

It is not surprising, then, that such teaching has created within evangelical churches a culture or ethos of activity. Charismatic renewal has added further fuel to the fire, as far as being busy for God is concerned.

The promise of spiritual power for service came as a welcome relief to many evangelicals. Worn out and drained by their constant service for God, and feeling ineffective and unfruitful, those who embraced the renewal movement found a welcome respite in the charismatic focus on 'baptism in the Spirit'. However, 40 years on, the evidence suggests that the charismatic movement has only intensified the pressure to do more.

Charismatic spirituality, along with the Church Growth Movement, has spurred on the existing belief in the possibility of numerical church growth. It has brought to us the importance of vision and strategy, of dreaming dreams about what God can do in our towns and cities. It has encouraged us to think big, to make plans, to have goals, to set ourselves targets. It has filled us with stories of large, successful churches and effective ministries. Church leaders, inspired and motivated by talk of revival and dreaming of similar success, willingly give themselves to even harder work, to accomplish their goals and achieve their ambitions. Congregations, too, are exhorted to commit themselves to big projects and to share the vision. For some, the dream comes true. For the majority, it is simply more treading of the treadmill.

Perhaps more than any other tradition, charismatic spirituality emphasises the part that men and women play in working with God. While many Christians claim to believe in the sovereignty of God, in practice most believe that everything depends on them. So it is that, strengthened by their understanding of the victory of Christ and their insights into spiritual warfare, many charismatics have turned their attention to world mission. The evangelisation of the nations is seen as a task that can be accomplished 'in our generation'. Such bold thinking has released into church life an even greater responsibility to work hard and achieve the task. There is a world to be saved and not much time in which to do it!

So here we have two spiritual traditions, both emphasising the importance of activity, and each influencing the other, so that the people within these traditions find themselves being constantly encouraged to do more for God. There is nothing intrinsically wrong with any of these emphases in themselves. It is their combined effect in increasing the push towards activity that gives concern.

There is no doubt that the most serious negative effect produced by this combination is performance-orientated living. For those of a tender conscience, repeated exhortations to work hard become internalised and lead to a 'drivenness' in behaviour. Such individuals feel guilty if they are not busy, and demonstrate an inability to relax or enjoy leisure time properly. They measure their relationship with God by how much they have done for him and only feel at peace when they feel they have done enough to satisfy this ever-demanding God. Ironically, this approach moves them out of grace-based living (the touchstone of evangelical teaching) into works-based living.

Pamela Evans has helpfully exposed this obsession with 'doing' in her challenging book, *Driven Beyond the Call of God*. She recognises that 'much of what passes for Christian fervour is workaholism with a religious gloss'.[20] She goes on to suggest that some forms of Christian activity are actually based on addictive patterns of behaviour, and she calls for us to rediscover a more balanced way of living, as described by Jesus in The Message's contemporary rendering of Matthew 11:29 as the 'unforced rhythms of grace'.

While drivenness has many roots, it seems to me that a major part of the problem is the lack of balance in evangelical/charismatic spirituality. We have a theology of work but not of rest, of doing but not of simply being. Pamela Evans' closing challenge is pertinent: '"Discovering the rhythms of grace" speaks to me of settling into the stride pattern we need in order to stay in step with him, neither lagging behind nor being driven beyond his call.'[21] It is certainly possible to be doing far more than God ever requires of us.

A second disturbing effect of spiritual activism is that we have no time simply to be still and enjoy God. Indeed, such spirituality can help us create an image of God that is far from attractive. It can generate in our minds a picture of one who is constantly demanding, hard to please, seldom satisfied and never off duty. Such a God is not easy to live with, even if we call him Father!

Furthermore, in this context, prayer itself is seen as work – in fact, as hard work. Gillett speaks of it as 'the intense energetic activity of evangelical intercessory prayer'.[22] Evangelicals emphasise this form of prayer because it is one of the means by which they get the work done. In order to see God in action, we must petition him to come to our aid. More than in any other tradition, intercessory prayer is exalted as the most important form of prayer. It often involves praying out loud, with great fervour and seriousness and for long periods of time. The idea of silent, contemplative prayer, of relaxing in God's presence and simply being with him without asking for anything, seems strange to many evangelicals. Gillett says, 'Personal spiritual growth may well be a by-product of this central evangelical prayer activity, but cultivation of one's own relationship with God is not the purpose of prayer as it is in some other traditions.'[23]

A third serious negative effect can be found in the damage to health, well-being and relationships that results from overactive lifestyles. Sadly, we may feel that this is the inevitable price we pay; this is how we show that we are committed. Increasing numbers of Christian workers are stressed out and suffering health problems; marriages are breaking down and children rebelling. Meanwhile, many are leaving the ministry and others are dropping out of the church, no longer able or willing to pay the price. Few seem willing to question this trend, to stand up and say, 'Wait a minute, this can't be right!' Organisations and churches go on demanding more and more from their people, not realising that they are driving them into the ground.

In the midst of it all, though, the still small voice of God can be heard, calling us back to balance and to the integration of quieter, more reflective ways. David Ellis, at the time UK Director of the Overseas Missionary Fellowship, made such a call in a very brave article called, appropriately, 'Why we may need to do less for God'. He likened some Christian workers to the workaholic, ambitious types found in secular employment, and said that hyperactivity has become an endemic disease in Christian circles. He also made this telling comment: 'Busyness takes over. Driven relentlessly without recognising the symptoms, we become infected by the disease of activism. It is easy to hide barrenness behind a charade of busyness; to rely on activity, plans, and strategies to cover spiritual bankruptcy.'[24]

But is there a solution? Ellis calls us back to the contemplative tradition and the 'waiting on God' which is at the heart of Christianity. He quotes Archbishop Michael Ramsey's reminder that St Dominic's great description of the Christian way was '*Contemplare et contemplata aliis tradere*': 'To contemplate and pass on to others the things contemplated'. Ramsey asked, 'Is our weakness in the second due to our being often too busy for the first?'

'Bob' is typical of many in Christian leadership. An exceptionally gifted individual, Bob was the International Director of a mission agency working in Africa. His job demanded a great deal of travel, a huge amount of public speaking and endless committees and councils. He threw himself wholeheartedly into his work, leading the mission through a process of change and transition to become more relevant to the contemporary world. He worked long hours and gave himself unstintingly. Eventually, though, the pace of his life and the demands upon him took their toll and he began to show all the classic signs of burn-out.

In order to recover, Bob was forced to take time off work. His doctor recommended medication and a reordering of his lifestyle. Bob himself began to rediscover the grace of God in the midst of his weakness and to realise that God loved him as much in his inactivity as in his busyness. This helped him to relax more and to slow down. Bob is back at work now, and, while the pressures are just as great, his priorities are different. He is learning to look after himself more, has a support group to curb his proneness to overcommit himself, and is giving more time to his relationship with God and the rhythms of grace in his own life.

Bob's story could be repeated countless times. It is the story of too many Christian workers and church leaders. It is an issue that we need to address. Evangelical activity and charismatic dynamism need the balance of contemplative stillness if we are to avoid further casualties. We may well need not only to do less for God, but also to do things differently. If we don't, we may well end up burned out on religion.

Learn from me

What is the Spirit saying to the Church at this time? Could it be that he is calling us to a greater balance in the way we live and minister? By looking at certain key biblical passages, and in particular the example and teaching of Jesus, we begin to see the need for a more balanced life – one that integrates the strengths of the contemplative tradition with a life of busy servanthood.

4

The example of Jesus

Was Jesus an activist? That is the picture we often have of him, at least from a simple reading of the gospels. His life was so full and so busy, with crowds demanding his attention and individuals wanting his help – always on the move, every day packed with incident and controversy. He was preaching the kingdom, healing the sick and answering questions, surrounded by people, bombarded with noise, constantly under pressure. He travelled from place to place, with never much privacy, nowhere really to call home and certainly no time to relax.

But was this really the way he lived his life? A closer examination reveals that Jesus was far more balanced in the way he handled himself and managed his time.

Reading the gospel story more carefully, we see that Jesus was never in a hurry and was always calm in his spirit. Far from being pressurised by the demands upon him, he seems to have made a habit of withdrawing from the hurly-burly in order to be alone with his Father. These interludes of 'aloneness' were integral to the way he lived and crucial to the maintenance of his relationship with the Father.

It is worth pointing out that Jesus was in no rush to begin his ministry. From his boyhood adventure in the temple to the beginning of his active ministry, we have a long period of silence, of hiddenness. His active ministry lasted only three years. Most of his life was spent in quiet obscurity, growing up in Nazareth, learning about himself and his ministry in the quiet Galilean backwater. It is worth noting, too, that when he revealed himself publicly at his baptism, the Father showed his approval of his Son: 'You are my Son, whom I love; with you I am well pleased' (Mark 1:11). This was before he had done anything to merit or earn such affirmation.

When eventually his ministry did get underway, it began with a Spirit-led period in the desert. We often assume that this was a negative period of spiritual conflict and hostility, but it seems probable that the temptations came at the end of the period in the desert: Matthew 4:2 says that it was after 40 days that he was hungry and the temptations began. So why did the Spirit lead Jesus into the wilderness? Presumably so that he could be alone with the Father and prepare himself for the ministry that lay ahead. Far from being a negative experience, this period was designed by the Spirit to be a positive time in which he could be built up and made ready for the challenges that faced him. Thus we read that Jesus 'returned to Galilee in the power of the Spirit' (Luke 4:14).

During the hectic period of ministry that followed, we can see Jesus carefully maintaining his relationship with the Father through times of strategic withdrawal. Even Mark's breathless account of those three years reveals this pattern: 'Very early in the morning, while it was still dark, Jesus got up, left the house and went off to a solitary place, where he prayed' (1:35). Despite the fact that everyone was looking for him (v. 37), Jesus disciplined himself to be alone. This solitude didn't happen without considerable cost and inconvenience, or without planning and forethought, but it was such a vital ingredient in his inner life that he could not manage without it.

We see the same resolve at other times in his ministry, and Luke regards it as part of a behaviour pattern: 'The news about him spread all the more, so that crowds of people came to hear him and to be healed of their sicknesses. But Jesus often withdrew to lonely places and prayed' (5:15–16). At crucial times in his ministry he would retire to be alone – for example, before choosing the apostles (Luke 6:12), after John the Baptist had died (Matthew 14:13), and before the transfiguration (17:1). More importantly, he sought time and space alone in the everyday demands of life, often walking by the lakeside (Mark 2:13; 3:7), withdrawing to the mountains (3:13; 6:46; 9:2) or enjoying the countryside (John 3:22). Walking through the fields as he journeyed from town to town provided quieter moments, and often, when the demands were great, a trip to the other side of the lake gave much-needed time alone (Matthew 8:18; 14:13). He had 'safe houses' that he could escape to (Mark 7:24), and friends like the trio at Bethany (Luke 10:38) who could offer him sanctuary.

Jesus did not avoid the crowds that demanded his attention, and he did not neglect his responsibilities, but he did guard enough of his time to maintain a living fellowship with his Father. David Runcorn notes, 'His disciples discovered that this regular withdrawal from people and activity was the one predictable thing about Jesus. He made silence and solitude his special companions. Whatever the demands upon him, he always found a time and space to hide away and be alone.'[25] So why was this kind of strategic withdrawal so important for Jesus?

Firstly, because he was human. Like anyone else, Jesus became tired by the constant demands of people and drained by the pressures of ministry. Being alone was a way of recharging himself, of nourishing his own spirit so that he could continue to give out to others. 'Time for oneself' is a basic human need and to deny or neglect it can lead to emotional, spiritual and physical breakdown. Thus we see Jesus sitting by the well of Sychar as the midday sun took its toll on him. Tired and thirsty, he sat down for a 'breather', allowing himself to rest and to be refreshed (John 4:6). His example liberates us to embrace our own humanity and gives us permission to rest.

The need for 'space' is not just a matter of personality or temperament. It is true that some people have a preference for aloneness (introverts), while others find stimulation and energy from doing things and being with people (extraverts). All of us, however, need time simply to be, when our spirits and souls can be recharged and refreshed. Introverts with busy jobs and lifestyles must ensure that they get sufficient time alone, and should not feel guilty when they need to withdraw from the hustle and bustle. Extraverts, because they get a buzz from activity, must be aware of their tendency to overcommit themselves and run on empty, making sure they discipline themselves to have quiet spells when they can replenish their inner resources.

A second reason that Jesus withdrew so often was because this was the way in which he maintained his relationship with the Father. He was alone not simply for peace and quiet but to commune with God. As David Runcorn puts it, 'In those lonely places the deep springs of the Spirit's life renewed him, the Father's will strengthened him and the Father's love inspired him.'[26] There in the stillness and silence he could hear God speak to him, and there he discovered the Father's will for his life. This, of course, was the secret of his ministry:

> 'I tell you the truth, the Son can do nothing by himself; he can do only what he sees the Father doing, because whatever the Father does the Son also does. For the Father loves the Son and shows him all he does… By myself I can do nothing; I judge only as I hear, and my judgment is just, for I seek not to please myself but him who sent me.'
> JOHN 5:19–20, 30

It was this secret place of communion with the Father that Jesus guarded so jealously. Since he was dependent on the Father to show him what to say and do, Jesus needed to stay in a place of intimacy, of close contact, of abiding. Out of this deep inner relationship flowed his life of fruitful ministry. No amount of busyness or legitimate demands were allowed to rob him of this place of oneness with the Father. His life was punctuated by a deliberate stopping of external activity in order to concentrate on the inner life of the spirit. Runcorn says, 'Punctuation is a helpful way of thinking about Jesus' relationship with silence and solitude… His times alone were the commas, pauses and full stops in the story of life. They gave the rest of his life its structure, direction and balance. His words and his works were born out of those hours of silent waiting upon God.'[27]

The implications of all this for ourselves are obvious. If Jesus needed to take time to be alone and find quietness for prayer, then so do we. If the secret of his effectiveness lay in maintaining a place of intimacy and communion with the Father, then that will be the way for us also. If he could stop and rest, so can we.

These times of rest will not happen automatically or without discipline on our part. We will need to value quietness far more than we do, and to understand the importance of 'aloneness' in developing our walk with God. It will require a change of mindset, from one that simply puts activity first to one that allows activity to flow out of relationship with the Father. Such a change, however, will bring enormous rewards: not only a healthier lifestyle but also a greater clarity in hearing the voice of God.

Jesus has given us an example so that we can follow in his steps. As we consider carefully how he lived and watch him in action, the Spirit calls us to imitate the Saviour and ensure a similar balance in our own lives.

5

'Come aside and be with me'

Not only did Jesus follow a pattern of strategic withdrawal in his own life, but he also encouraged it in the lives of his followers. They could see for themselves, by his example, that it was a priority for him. Jesus, however, took the principle further by actively calling them to experience silence and solitude for themselves.

The occasion came early in the ministry of Jesus, but the crowds were already gathering and the momentum was beginning. The disciples had been sent out by Jesus in pairs for their first taste of ministry, and had returned buoyed up by their success. At the same time, news had just arrived of the death of John the Baptist. Probably because of his own need to get away at such an emotional time, and also because it was a crucial moment to teach his disciples a foundational lesson, Jesus called them to join in a strategic withdrawal. The full account is given in Mark 6:30–32.

To those newly involved in ministry, busyness is a welcome pressure. It gives the feeling of being wanted, of being used by God, of being successful. It creates a good impression, too, in the eyes of other people. The disciples were certainly busy. They had much to say about what they had already done on their recent ministry trip. Now they were in constant demand from many different quarters, with people coming and going all day long. So busy were they that they had no time even to eat. There was a buzz about the place, and the disciples were loving it.

To their surprise, Jesus called them to drop everything and follow him to the desert (Mark 6:32). It must have been puzzling to the disciples to be told to 'down tools' just as things were beginning to happen. Jesus, however, had a different agenda and something important to teach them if they were to be successful in ministry over the long term. Already he could see a worrying trend in what they were doing. This was the second time they had been unable to eat (see Mark 3:20), and a workaholic, needs-driven ministry was not the kind of service he either modelled or approved. It was time for them to learn the lesson of a balanced lifestyle. Driven on by their own success and facing the unrelenting needs of people, the disciples would soon wear themselves out unless they learned how to care for themselves.

'Come with me,' says Jesus. The call to discipleship is, first and foremost, a call to be in fellowship and friendship with Jesus. How easy it is to let the demands of ministry squeeze out those times of closeness with him. We end up working for him rather than being with him. When he first called the disciples, the priority was clear: first, to be with him; second, to be sent out by him (Mark 3:14). That order was in danger of being reversed, to the detriment of the disciples themselves and those whom they sought to help.

'Come… by yourselves.' Jesus wants his disciples to be with him. He values them for who they are, not what they do, and desires to enjoy their company. This means that they must leave the work behind and separate themselves from other people. Letting go is never easy. The need to be needed is very great and is deeply motivational. Success, once achieved, is not something that we easily risk losing. It can seem more prudent to work than to rest.

'Come… to a quiet place.' Quite literally, Jesus invites his followers into a desert place – not to what they might immediately regard as a beautiful place or even an interesting one, but to a very lonely place. It's remote, isolated, solitary, barren. There, free from distractions (even the distractions of legitimate work and deserving people), they can learn together how to spend time in God's presence and learn together how to hear his still, small voice.

'Come... and get some rest.' 'The bow that is never unstrung will quickly break,' said John Chrysostom (the fourth-century Archbishop of Constantinople), echoing the wisdom of Jesus. The master can see the need for his disciples to build into their hectic schedules periods of rest and refreshment. He calls for a divinely sanctioned 'intermission'. The Greek word used (*anapauo*) means 'to cause to rest' (body), 'to soothe' (soul), and 'to refresh' (spirit). It carries the sense of being renewed in every area of one's being. This is the 'real rest' that Jesus wants to give to all (Matthew 11:29). How important, then, that his representatives are living in the good of it themselves. Worn-out, weary and exhausted believers are not a good recommendation for the gospel of rest.

'So they went away by themselves in a boat to a solitary place' (v. 32). How thankful Jesus must have been for that boat! Time and again we read in the gospels how he got into the boat and they rowed to the other side of the lake. It was his way of finding peace and quiet, his means of escape. The disciples, whether willingly or not, followed him. They were not always quick to learn, and the lesson that communion with God precedes service for God has never been an easy one for any generation to grasp.

The habit that Jesus sought to build into the lives of the first apostles is sometimes resisted today. The idea of 'withdrawal', even strategic withdrawal, seems too defensive for some and defeatist to others. It is, however, part of a balanced and healthy spiritual life. If we are to breathe out, we must first breathe in. There is a natural rhythm to living the Christian life, which William Barclay notes in his commentary on this passage: 'Here we see what might be called the rhythm of the Christian life. For the Christian life is a continuous going into the presence of God from the presence of men, and coming into the presence of men from the presence of God. It is like the rhythm of work and sleep.'[28]

Barclay goes on to point out that there are two dangers in life. The first is the danger of too much activity, and the second is that of too much withdrawal. Then he suggests the proper balance with these words: 'The rhythm of the Christian life is the alternate meeting with God in the secret place and serving man in the market place.'[29]

Barclay is right when he emphasises the need for balance. We need both engagement and withdrawal. The danger in today's Christianity, however, is an overemphasis on activity. As we see Jesus teaching his disciples to value the 'quiet' life, we again hear the Spirit calling us to take time to be with the Master. Barclay concludes:

> It may well be that the whole trouble in our lives is that we give God no opportunity to speak to us, because we do not know how to be still and to listen; we give God no time to recharge us with spiritual energy and strength, because there is no time when we wait upon him. How can we shoulder life's burdens if we have no contact with him who is the Lord of all good life? How can we do God's work unless in God's strength? And how can we receive that strength unless we seek, in quietness and in loneliness, the presence of God?[30]

6

Learning to sit

A striking illustration of the importance that Jesus gave to the contemplative dimension occurs during one of his frequent visits to the home of his good friends, Mary and Martha. Their home in Bethany was undoubtedly one of the 'safe houses' where Jesus found a haven from the increasing demands of public ministry. However, it was not always an oasis of peace and quiet, as the story in Luke 10:38–42 reveals.

Perhaps, on this occasion, Jesus and his disciples arrive unexpectedly and unannounced. Martha, always keen to welcome her guests and look after them properly, is thrown into a panic and begins hurriedly making preparations in the kitchen. Mary, on the other hand, is less flappable than her sister and chooses to sit at the feet of Jesus and listen to what he has to share. It is not long before Martha's sense of injustice boils over into outrage. She has been left (again?) to do all the work and she feels wronged by her sister. Indignantly, she appeals to Jesus to tell Mary to help her.

We may well feel a great deal of sympathy for Martha. She has a fair point and we expect Jesus to adjudicate in her favour. She is, after all, acting in line with her culture; Mary is the radical one, overturning the conventions of the day by not getting involved in serving her guests. But no, to our surprise, he takes Mary's side. Mary is the one who has made the right choice. To sit and listen to what the Master has to say is what counts. Martha, with all her customary busyness and desire to please, has allowed herself to be distracted. She has actually missed the main point. This particular guest is not so concerned with being served as with being listened to. It is Martha's attention that he wants, not her activity.

What appears to be an ordinary domestic dispute has a much more profound significance. It is really about two different approaches to the Christian life. Martha represents 'the life of busy servanthood', while Mary typifies 'the life of quiet contemplation'. Both are important but one must have priority. According to Jesus, sitting and listening to what he has to say must come before dashing around in service.

The evangelical and charismatic sections of the church have largely adopted Martha's pattern of busy servanthood, characterised by activity and doing, serving and caring and helping, campaigning and protesting. It expresses itself through meetings and committees, with projects and programmes and by initiatives and endeavours. It is summed up in visions and goals and measured in objectives and achievements. It requires a great deal of effort, and those who live this way must be highly committed.

The life of quiet contemplation is very different. It is about being rather than doing, about becoming rather than achieving. It expresses itself through reflection, meditation and contemplation. It requires quietness and stillness, time and space, solitude and silence. It is about listening rather than talking, resting rather than working, receiving rather than giving. It requires just as much commitment and effort, but in a different way, allowing God to be God and waiting for him to act.

The life of busy servanthood has, of course, good biblical precedent. Just before this incident, Jesus had told the parable of the good Samaritan, which ends with a challenge to 'go and do likewise' (Luke 10:37). Many of us have heard that word and, ever since, have been 'going' and 'doing'. Unfortunately, we have not always heard the other word that calls us to sit and listen. We have become distracted and have neglected our fellowship with Jesus.

As we saw earlier, evangelical/charismatic spirituality values busyness. Busyness makes us feel good. It gives us the impression that we are achieving something, that we are going somewhere. We may actually be achieving very little and going round in circles, but at least we are doing something. Churches described as 'alive' have busy programmes, and 'active' Christians are involved in everything.

The result is an increasing number of highly committed Christians who are stressed out by trying to balance the demands of home, work and church. Luke the physician accurately diagnoses Martha's 'hurry sickness'.[31] She is 'distracted' (literally, wheeling about, overbusied), 'worried' (literally, anxious and careworn) and 'upset' (literally, troubled, disturbed, in a state of mental agitation). It's not a pretty picture but, sadly, it is an accurate description of many in the contemporary church, especially the leaders.

What we need to do is to balance our natural tendency to activism with a rediscovery of contemplative spirituality, a return to the practice of sitting at the feet of Jesus. How can this happen?

Firstly, we must stop. For those addicted to a busy lifestyle, this may be a frightening thought, but it is essential that we learn the discipline of stopping. We must take time out of busy schedules to be quiet and alone with God. We need enough time to switch off from daily demands and switch on to God again. We must rediscover the value of daily times alone with God, of sabbath rest, of quiet days and retreats.

Secondly, we must learn simply to sit – to learn how to rest without feeling guilty, and to rest not just physically but inwardly, too. We need to find the sabbath rest that still awaits the people of God (Hebrews 4:9) – a rest that comes from letting God take the strain in our lives and ministries. To enter God's rest, we must cease from our own labours. It is God's work, after all, and the responsibility rightly belongs on his shoulders.

Thirdly, we must listen. When our hearts are quiet and the noise of our own activity has ceased, we will again hear the voice of God. His word is life and light. When he speaks, we know what we should be doing. Work commissioned by God carries its own blessing and authentication. We may indeed end up doing less, but what we do will be more fruitful and not so exhausting.

Jesus commended Mary because she had 'chosen what is better' (Luke 10:42). There is a choice to be made, and what we choose is important. It is not an 'either/or' choice, however, but rather a question of which comes first – what is foundational. In spiritual terms, work proceeds from a place of rest. Our busy servanthood must be underpinned by quiet contemplation. The challenge is to ensure that we give due attention to this part of our lives.

'It will not be taken away from her' (v. 42). The fruits of contemplation are seen in the transformation of our inner lives, the formation of character, the shaping of attitudes and the internalising of values. These are lasting benefits. Activity may or may not produce results. Being with Jesus certainly will.

Once more we hear the call of the Spirit. There in the house at Bethany, he beckons us to a greater intimacy with the Master. To sit at his feet and listen: this is what the Lord requires.

7

Bearing fruit the natural way

For several years I had a poster in my office that showed a picture of St George slaying the dragon. Underneath were these words: 'What will you be remembered for?' It is an important question. We all know what St George is remembered for, but what kind of a legacy will we leave behind? What will people say about us when our life is over? What impact will we have made on the world?

Christians, above all, should be concerned to make their lives count, to live 'on purpose'. Part of that purpose is clearly that we should give our lives to serving God and sharing in his eternal purpose for the world. Many of us have given ourselves energetically and enthusiastically to this goal, and we are living 'purpose-driven lives', to the delight of American pastor Rick Warren.[32] We do so gladly and willingly, for this is part of what it means to be a follower of Jesus, who said to his disciples, 'You did not choose me, but I chose you and appointed you to go and bear fruit – fruit that will last' (John 15:16).

I can still remember clearly the day when, as a 15-year-old boy, I became conscious for the first time that God was calling me to himself. There in the tiny Methodist chapel in the village where I had grown up, God broke into my life. Almost immediately, I knew as well that he wanted me to serve him. It seemed to be part of the deal. I wasn't sure exactly how I would serve him, but I knew I had to give my whole life to him, and that he had a plan and purpose for me.

Jesus made it clear that God wants our lives to bear fruit for him. If we are truly his disciples, there will be some tangible expression of service in our lives: 'This is to my Father's glory, that you bear much fruit, showing yourselves to be my disciples' (John 15:8). So it is that any believer who takes seriously the claims of Christ on their life will be involved in some form of Christian service. It is both the Father's wish and the disciple's desire, and most of us set about the task of living for Jesus with an abundance of zeal and determination.

It is just here, though, that the problem lies. Firstly, we often throw ourselves into Christian ministry with our own human zeal and natural energy. It sometimes takes many tiring years of effort and lots of painful failures before we finally come to an end of ourselves and begin to learn one of the most important spiritual lessons of all – that apart from Christ we can do nothing (John 15:5).

More than that, our very focus on doing things for God gets in the way of what ought to be a priority for us and is, in any case, the secret of fruitfulness in ministry – our relationship with him. We often become immersed in worthwhile activity and so committed to the cause that we neglect our fellowship with God, the very thing that would ensure our effectiveness.

Jesus was at great pains to instruct his disciples that if they wanted to bear fruit that would stand the test of time, they would do so only if they stayed in living contact with himself. He likened the relationship to the way a branch remains in the vine and so bears fruit naturally and easily. The secret of a fruitful life is just as simple: we are to remain in Christ. He says, 'I am the Vine, you are the branches. When you're joined with me and I with you, the relation intimate and organic, the harvest is sure to be abundant. Separated, you can't produce a thing' (John 15:5, *The Message*).

We don't have to work ourselves to the bone or drive ourselves into the dust in order to bear fruit for God. It isn't about doing more, trying harder or redoubling our efforts. The secret lies in being connected to Jesus in a living, vital relationship. In other words, the key to effective service is deeper intimacy, not increased activity.

Bruce Wilkinson is a respected Bible teacher and leader of an international Christian organisation in America. Some years ago, he reached a point in his ministry where, although he was outwardly successful, inwardly he was running on empty. His passion for ministry seemed to have gone and, although he was working harder than ever, he had less satisfaction than at any time in his life. In desperation, he went to talk with a respected mentor and friend.

Their conversation soon revealed the cause of his problem: he had been neglecting his relationship with God. Painfully the truth dawned on him: 'God didn't want me to do more *for* him. He wanted me to be more *with* him.'[33] The whole experience led Wilkinson to a new appreciation of abiding (or remaining) in Christ and a new level of fruitfulness in ministry, which he has since been able to share with thousands around the world. He saw that he must make intimacy with God his *first* priority. He writes, 'His purpose is not that you will do more for him but that you will choose to be more with him. Only by abiding can you enjoy the most rewarding friendship with God and experience the greatest abundance for his glory.'[34]

Friendship is what it is all about, and we have to make room for that friendship in our busy schedules. If necessary, we have to trim our lives of distractions and alternatives, however praiseworthy they may be, in order to prioritise our relationship with Jesus. The relationship then becomes the source of our spiritual vitality, and we begin to live out of it. In this way, his life begins to operate in us rather than our own, and we experience what some have called the 'exchanged life' – Christ living his life in us and through us.

Intimacy, of course, requires the investment of quality time. As Andrew Murray has said, 'It takes time to grow into Jesus the Vine; do not expect to abide in him unless you will give him that time.'[35] We take time to pray, to worship, to soak up his word, to dwell in his presence, to listen for his voice. We have time to linger, to relax, to be with him without any agenda, to enjoy him without making any demands. Later in this book, we will look at practical ways by which we can abide, but we must always remember that abiding is about being with a person, not mastering a formula or technique. Steve McVey puts it very clearly when he says:

> Abiding in Christ isn't achieved by successfully following certain steps. It's an act of faith by which we simply choose to believe that he is our life, that he will express himself through us, and then act as if he is doing that very thing at this very moment. Abundant living isn't found in a plan, but in the person of Jesus Christ. That fact can't be overstated or emphasised too many times.[36]

If we want to learn to abide in Christ, we needn't worry about the right or wrong way to do it. We simply make it our aim to be with Jesus and enjoy his friendship, and the rest will take care of itself. We come into his presence and dwell in his love (John 15:9), make ourselves at home in his acceptance of us, and allow ourselves to be filled again with his life. This is the essence of abiding.

We have seen in Chapter 4 that Jesus was effective in ministry because he took time to abide in his Father's love, continually escaping from the pressures and demands in order to be renewed and refreshed by time alone with him. As we watch Jesus at work, we learn how to work with him. His example becomes our pattern. If it worked for him, it will work for us.

As we learn to abide, we will discern more clearly exactly what God wants us to do. So much of our work is ineffective because it is simply a good idea on our part rather than an idea originating in God. As we wait on God, we are better able to hear what he is saying and become more attentive to his voice. We begin to recognise more readily the Spirit's promptings and are more responsive to his leading. Then our only concern is to obey. If we are hearing God's voice and doing his will, our work is far more likely to be fruitful.

Not only that, but as we dwell in his presence, we are energised by the Spirit and strengthened for the task. Rather than being constantly drained because we are working in our own energy, we learn how to operate from the strength of Christ within us. We discover the 'rest' of God – the sense of relaxation that enhances everything we do. Rather than being uptight and on edge (the mark of human effort), we are relaxed and natural (the mark of God at work in us). Thus we work both more efficiently and more effectively. By doing less, we may actually end up doing more.

The branch takes no credit for producing fruit: the life of the vine does that. The branch's only responsibility is to stay joined to the vine, and then fruit-bearing is natural and easy. Likewise, if we desire to bear fruit for God, our only responsibility is to stay in union with Christ and respond to the movement of his life within us. Thus we can live freely and lightly, bearing fruit the easy way.

8

Centred on Jesus

'Eccentric.' Few of us would appreciate such a description, but that is what many of us are. The word means to be 'off-centre', and, when it comes to the way we live our lives, a good number of us could justifiably be described as 'off-centre'. Although the Christian life is meant to be lived with Jesus at the centre, our busyness and focus on activity have often relegated him to the circumference of our lives.

Michael Frye's compelling song 'Jesus, be the centre' resonates with many people simply because they recognise that they are living 'eccentrically' and yearn for something better.[37] They long for Jesus to be the source of their life, to be their hope, their guide. This modern-day psalm expresses exactly the anguished heart-cry of many contemporary children of God who yearn to put Jesus back at the centre of life.

The writer to the Hebrews shared a similar sentiment. His letter was written with the aim of encouraging first-century believers to keep on believing, despite the pressures. They were in danger of drifting away, letting go their grip and throwing away their confidence. Some had already stopped meeting for fellowship; others were getting tangled up in sin again. Most disconcertingly, they had begun to lose their focus on Jesus.

Into this context the writer speaks with clarity and conviction, calling the believers back to a Christ-centred faith: 'Let us fix our eyes on Jesus,' he urges (Hebrews 12:2). Whatever the pressures, whatever the distractions, this is the answer. Take another look at Jesus; fix your gaze upon him. Such a preoccupation was more than adequate to cure the malady of soul that had overtaken those Hebrew Christians. The answer to the pull of sin is not greater discipline, stricter rules or trying harder. It is to fall in love with Jesus all over again.

Athletic contests were popular throughout the ancient world. Using imagery that would have been very familiar to his readers, the writer to the Hebrews likens the Christian life to a race, and the believers to runners who have become exhausted, in danger of collapsing before the finishing line. He says that they are 'weary' and about to 'lose heart' (v. 3), a description that aptly summarises the way many people feel in church today.

'Weary' translates a Greek word that means 'to tire with exertion, to labour to the point of weariness, to feel exhausted, to become sick'. The second expression, 'lose heart', is literally 'fainting in the souls of you', suggesting despondency, a condition of being mentally weary, having nothing left to give any more, and having lost all creativity. Today we would call this 'burn-out', and the symptoms are all too familiar to those of us who have pastoral care of church leaders, missionaries and people who work in Christian organisations. If we are to recover our lives, we need to come to Jesus and learn from him. We need to fix our eyes once more upon him.

The writer calls us to 'consider' Jesus (v. 3), just as he earlier encourages us to 'fix our eyes on' him (v. 2). The word 'consider' means 'to look carefully at, to gaze upon, to look with loving attentiveness'. The word is sometimes used of astronomers who gaze at the heavens with diligence and concentration, and it reminds me of a young man I read about who was watching the stars one night through his home-made telescope. Such was the intensity and carefulness of his gaze that he spotted a star that had never been seen before. His discovery was verified and he was given the honour of naming the newly identified star. What concentration! What dedication to star-gazing! If we are to shake off our spiritual lethargy and cure our spiritual exhaustion, what are we to do? Nothing, except to look lovingly and adoringly at Jesus. We are to turn our eyes upon him, deliberately and definitely making him the centre of our attention.

King David, in the Old Testament, knew the benefit and blessing of worshipping God and, in the context of worship, allowing his gaze to rest on the Lord. That is why, in Psalm 27, we read that his lifelong prayer was this: 'One thing I ask of the Lord, this is what I seek: that I may dwell in the house of the Lord all the days of my life, to gaze upon the beauty of the Lord and to seek him in his temple' (v. 4). This warrior king, this 'man after God's own heart', had only one real desire. He longed to know God more intimately, to be more at home in his presence, to appreciate more fully his beauty.

This is the only biblical reference to 'the beauty of the Lord', and it is an unusual expression – the language of love and devotion rather than theology and doctrine. We are more accustomed to speaking about the attributes of God, analysing his qualities and systematising his activities, than to feeling his attractiveness and his desirability. 'Beauty' takes us into another realm altogether – the subjective, affective realm where emotions are real and valued.

'The beauty of the Lord' is an attempt to describe the overall impact or impression that the Lord, in his completeness, makes upon those who encounter him. It tries to sum up the feelings generated by the totality of who God is. When we meet God in the person of Jesus, we experience beauty – sheer loveliness, tenderness, compassion, charm and grace. Words are inadequate to convey what is felt, what is known intuitively. Once we have experienced it, however, we are refreshed, renewed and revitalised. We thirst for more of him, and we do so with the assurance that if we seek him, we shall find him; if we have a longing for him, it will eventually be satisfied.

David and the Old Testament prophets (such as Isaiah, Jeremiah and Habakkuk) knew what it was to wait on God. They knew how to linger in his presence and seek his face in quiet, contemplative prayer. They knew themselves to be dependent upon God, and they were content to wait for God to reveal himself, to act in his own chosen time. There in the secret place, they discovered true rest: 'Find rest, O my soul, in God alone; my hope comes from him. He alone is my rock and my salvation; he is my fortress, I will not be shaken' (Psalm 62:5–6).

When the writer to the Hebrews calls us to 'fix our eyes upon Jesus', he is asking for the same contemplative approach. We are to allow the Spirit to make Jesus real to us and, through our worship, prayer and meditation, allow ourselves to be recentred. He takes the fragmented pieces of our lives and puts them back together again. As we wait on the Lord, we find that our strength is renewed. We are able to mount up like eagles, carried on the currents of divine love and grace, held aloft by the sustaining wind of the Spirit. Then it is that we are empowered to run and not grow weary, to walk and never faint (see Isaiah 40:27–31).

As we allow our eyes to return to Jesus, we also look once more to the cross and are reminded of all he has done for us there. We allow our minds to be filled again with the wonder of everything his saving death has accomplished for us. We have been reconciled to the Father, totally forgiven of all our sins (past, present and future) and brought back into a permanent love-relationship with him. As we meditate on these foundational truths, the joy and delight of who we are in Christ and all that is ours in him can begin to flood our hearts and minds again. Our souls are restored, our faith is refreshed and our hope is rekindled.

More than that, as we gaze upon him, we notice where he is – seated at God's right hand, enthroned in heaven. He is the one who died but rose again and ascended victoriously. From this place of rule and authority, he is now able to pour his grace into our lives moment by moment and day by day (Hebrews 4:14–16). Fortified by this gift of divine strength, we are more able to cope with the pressures and trials of life. Strangely, this infusion of grace comes about when we give up our futile struggle to overcome by our own efforts and, instead, do nothing but wait upon God. It is almost as if God were waiting for us to come to an end of ourselves in order that his divine life might take over.

Here again we see the wonder of divine grace and the invitation to intimacy. It is not offered to the deserving as a reward for successful living, but to the needy to sustain them in their weakness. That is why we need not fear to draw near. We will not be rejected or shut out. We will meet with mercy, not judgment; with acceptance, not condemnation. We can come just as we are and find grace to help us in our time of need.

At this point, the contemplative dimension moves us back into the activist realm, for there is a race to be run and there is a course marked out for each of us. Looking to Jesus provides us with the inspiration to run the race. The contemplative is again seen to be the bedrock of the practical. This race is no saunter along country lanes, either, but a vigorous marathon that takes us through rough and rugged terrain. The road ahead of us has its ups and downs, its twists and its turns. It is both exhilarating and dangerous. Many surprises await us; many challenges will meet us on the way. We need stamina, determination and guts – all that the writer to the Hebrews means by 'perseverance' (12:1). To do the will of God in the world today is not easy, for it takes us to the hardest of places and to people in the greatest of need. There is often opposition, always temptation. We will be stretched to the limit if we follow Jesus, but never overwhelmed if our eyes remain fixed on him.

The key to running well and finishing the course lies in our being centred on him. As Andrew Murray puts it:

> *Looking to Jesus,*
> *with the look of faith, because salvation is in him alone;*
> *with the look of love, because he alone can satisfy the heart;*
> *with the look of strong desire, longing to know him better;*
> *with the look of soul devotion, waiting only to know his will;*

with the look of gladness, because we know he loves us;
with the look of wonder and admiration, for he is the brightness
of the Father's glory, our Lord and our God.[38]

Whatever our calling, and wherever it takes us, we can do no better
than this.

Get away with me

The invitation to intimacy that Jesus gives us inevitably involves a call to be alone with him. The pressures of life do not make this easy to do, and nor does the ethos of contemporary evangelical and charismatic Christianity, obsessed as it is with activity and achievement. However, we are recognising increasingly the importance of having a greater balance in the way we live the Christian life. Those of us who are busy activists need to build into our lives more time and space for God. If we are to do this, we must learn how to be still, and then how to listen quietly to God. Although we may be able to do this in the company of others, it will be better achieved through times of being alone. Stillness, silence and solitude are the basic ingredients of contemplative spirituality, and it is to an examination of these factors that we now turn. While they belong together and overlap with each other, for the sake of clarity we will look at each in turn.

9

Stillness

I remember reading to my children a very popular book called *Richard Scarry's Busy, Busy World*. Every colourful page was a mass of detail, with all kinds of characters doing all kinds of things. The children pored over each page, fascinated by the variety, and never tired of talking about what they saw. Without realising it, of course, I was introducing them to the idea that the world is a very busy place and that everyone who lives there ought to be busy, too.

We cannot isolate ourselves from the demands of daily living. The world is indeed a busy place, and it is getting busier all the time. Rather than creating more leisure time, technology has increased the pace of life. Quicker transportation and faster communication, in particular, have speeded things up, so that we are expected to do more in a shorter space of time. Inevitably we become caught up in the whirl of activity and movement that surrounds us, and find ourselves living to the beat and rhythm of a society that is increasingly wound up. In such a context it is extremely difficult to slow down and adopt a gentler tempo.

We have our own internal pressures, too. We want to succeed, to make progress, to do well. We have an inbuilt need to achieve and to prove ourselves, to create the right impression and live up to the expectations of other people. Christians can be as competitive as anyone and equally as keen to outdo their counterparts (we would not call them rivals). However much we would like to think that the motivation for our Christian service is entirely pure, in reality we can be moved as strongly by our need to achieve and to make our mark as by a desire to glorify God.

In such a context, the very idea of slowing down, let alone stopping, becomes threatening and risky. If we let up on our busyness, even for a moment, will we fall behind in the race? If we ease up on our schedules and do less, will we fail to reach our targets? If we are still, how can we achieve? And yet we know that if we are to experience God in a deeper way, we will have to make time and space to be with him.

Ken Blanchard is the author of *The One-Minute Manager* and a leading management consultant. In an article entitled 'Don't work harder – work smarter', he highlights one of the important lessons of leadership: 'Most people mentally have a sign on their desk that reads: Don't just sit there, do something! The best advice I ever received was to redo the sign to read: Don't just do something, sit there!'[39]

Psalm 46 contains one of the most compelling reasons for learning to be still. God himself is speaking, at a time when society is in turmoil and even the most stable elements are giving way. This is his exhortation: 'Be still, and know that I am God' (Psalm 46:10). We can know God to a certain degree and at a certain level in the midst of our activity and busyness, but the more intimate knowledge of God is reserved for those who will quieten themselves and be still before him. It is this deeper knowledge of God that will keep us stable through times of turmoil and change, as Psalm 46 indicates.

When I speak here about knowing God, I am talking about what we call 'revelation' knowledge – an awareness that goes beyond the facts we know about God in our heads and becomes the truth that grips us in our hearts. This kind of revelation, in my experience, usually comes in moments when I am relaxed in God's presence, when I have taken the time to sit and be still and to wait on God. Then it is that some particular insight will come to me. Stillness seems to be a prerequisite for such revelation, because it creates the environment in which our spirit becomes more receptive to God and attuned to his Spirit.

This 'stillness of soul' is further described for us in Psalm 131. Here the psalmist approaches God in humility and deliberately quietens himself before the Lord: 'But I have stilled and quietened myself, just as a small child is quiet with its mother. Yes, like a small child is my soul within me' (v. 2, NLT). Through this tender imagery, we can see what is involved in the process of stilling ourselves. We can picture a fractious child, screaming and crying, agitated and distressed. Then perhaps comes the succour and comfort of the mother's breast, the feeling of closeness, the awareness of being embraced by love. Gradually the child quietens and becomes content. Instead of wriggling and writhing, the little body stills, and presently is asleep.

According to the psalmist, this is something we must learn to do before God. Often we come to him in a state of agitation and distress. We are troubled and anxious. We are wound up inside, coiled like a spring, full of inner tension. Our greatest need is to be able to relax ourselves, but how can we do this? By resting in God's great love for us and allowing him to succour us. As we consciously still ourselves and begin drawing on the great truths of his mercy and grace, reminding ourselves of his sovereign control, his peace begins to flow into our troubled minds. This doesn't happen instantaneously or automatically. It takes time. It requires that we discipline our mind and our emotions. Gradually, however, a stillness of soul creeps over us and, with it, the contentedness that makes it easier for us to 'know' our God.

For all this to happen, we have to nurture an outer stillness. This means that we have to separate ourselves from our work and activity and from legitimate demands on our time, even for a short period. It is not always easy to achieve but, with self-discipline and good planning, it is possible to make time even in the busiest of diaries.

Evangelicals are familiar with the idea of a daily 'quiet time'. Unfortunately, this time often has very little 'quiet' within it. It tends to be given to Bible reading and 'shopping list' prayer – both worthwhile activities, but activities just the same. With a little adaptation, the framework of a regular quiet time can provide an ideal opportunity for stillness and a silent waiting upon God.

For those who do not follow such a regular pattern, it is important to set aside quality time to be with God and to practise the discipline of stopping. I worked at a Christian conference centre where we had a daily mid-morning time of prayer. It was surprising how strong the temptation was to skip this time, especially when the workload was heavy. It requires a measure of faith to stop and spend time with God. We need to recognise the value and importance of these times, realising that they will not happen by chance or by accident: we have to make them happen. Even 15 minutes of stillness on a regular basis (daily, if possible) can provide an oasis of calm and refreshment.

Graham and Jo are both busy people, but, even when their children were small, they were determined to find a quiet place amid the hurly-burly of family life. They erected a little shed in their garden and used it in turns each morning as a place of escape from the noise and pressure of their daily lives. It became an oasis for them and provided the opportunity to find stillness with God.

For some people, the taking of a regular Quiet Day has provided the necessary breathing space in a hectic schedule – perhaps one day every month or every quarter, reserved in order to get away to a quiet place and be alone with God. The venue is important. It should be a place where you can feel relaxed and undisturbed. Being surrounded by beautiful countryside is helpful for many, and buildings with a prayerful and peaceful atmosphere make it easier to seek God. Such a day can be taken alone or in the company of others.

Jonathan is the leader of a growing church in the north of England. He is the kind of person who involves himself in everything that is going on and is always ready to respond to the needs of others. Increasingly he has realised, however, the importance of having time and space for himself. Now he sets aside in his diary a day each month for reading and reflection. He travels to a nearby Christian centre and finds a quiet corner in the library where he can be undisturbed. It is his way of making sure his life does not become overbusy and that he has quality time with God.

More and more of us are finding it helpful to go on retreat and spend several days away from the normal daily demands in order to be with God and nurture our inner life. There are a growing number of retreat centres and programmes on offer to meet this need. For some people, however, the idea of a retreat sounds a defeatist note. As someone said to me, 'I don't want to retreat, brother, I want to advance!' Perhaps, if we think of a retreat as a 'strategic withdrawal' (as I have already suggested), it will make more sense to those for whom it is a difficult term: essentially, a retreat is an opportunity to withdraw for a while in order to gain perspective and be renewed for the ongoing battle.[40]

Having made space and time for God, we still have to deal with the process of 'winding down', which may not come at all easily to the more hyperactive among us. Even being physically still can be a challenge for someone who is restlessly on the go, and most energetic people find that it takes a while to slow down properly. A comfortable chair will help, of course, and some basic relaxation techniques. Wanda Nash, an experienced retreat leader, has written helpfully in *Christ, Stress and Glory* about the place of breath control in helping us to relax.[41] In contemplative terminology, this is called 'centring' oneself. She also gives an excellent description of how to spend a short time being still with God.

To put her recommendations simply, it is a matter of learning to breathe more slowly. As we find a place to relax ourselves, such as lying on the floor, we can let our breathing slow down until we begin to breathe automatically, from the belly rather than from the chest. As we do this, we soon find the body's natural rhythm, which may be much slower than we are used to. Presently, the rest of the body comes to stillness and we find ourselves at peace. This is a good technique to use when sleep is difficult or we are feeling tense about something.

Another technique that has proven value is the use of a 'rhythm' prayer. Here, a very simple prayer is repeated over and over again in rhythm with the breathing. The most well-known is the Jesus Prayer,[42] which has been used for centuries. As you breathe in, you pray (either silently or aloud), 'Jesus Christ, Son of God', and then, as you breathe out, '… have mercy on me'. As well as being a very profound prayer, the rhythmic repetition has a calming effect. It is recommended that you sit very still, with palms raised towards God in a receptive gesture. These are not magical words, however: we can substitute other words that are just as scriptural and may meet our situation more appropriately at a particular moment – for example, 'Spirit of the living God… fall afresh on me' or 'Father in heaven… hallowed be your name.'

If outer stillness is difficult to achieve, inner stillness can be even more elusive. We may find ourselves sitting quietly in some beautiful setting but with a great restlessness swirling around inside us. For those of us who are evangelicals, it seems important to give ourselves permission to be still, and this means having good scriptural warrant for being what we might call 'inactive' or 'off-duty'. Without this permission, we tend to be plagued by guilt and find it impossible to rest or relax. This is where a proper understanding of the sabbath principle can come to our aid.

Far from being merely a piece of restrictive legislation, the command to keep a sabbath (Exodus 20:8–11) enshrines a vital spiritual truth: God worked for six days, and then rested (Genesis 2:2–3). The call to keep a sabbath was a call to enter into the rest of God, to stop our own activity and focus on him, and to share his satisfaction in a job well done.

Not surprisingly, this call to rest and cease from our own activities, even for one day, meets with resistance in our society. Commerce and business cannot wait; sport and leisure demand our time. Sunday has become a day like any other, full of busyness and activity. In rejecting the call for a sabbath, we have rejected the need for stillness and rest, and we are poorer as a result. Christians have suffered as much as anyone from this, by allowing themselves to follow the trends of today's world and in their failure to keep a true day of rest.[43]

However, behind the call for a specific day of rest is a more urgent and pressing call to rest in God. This is the true sabbath, in which we allow God his rightful place in our lives and trust him, in creaturely dependence, to do everything for us. It is a difficult lesson to learn, for our nature is to be independent of God and to act out of our own strength and effort to solve our problems and achieve our goals. Stopping our own activities and becoming still is therefore an act of faith in which we express our trust in God to work on our behalf. Richard Foster has written:

> No teaching flowing out of the Sabbath principle is more important than the centrality of our resting in God. Instead of striving to make this or that happen, we learn to trust in a heavenly Father who loves to give. This does not promote inactivity, but it does promote dependent activity. No longer do we take things into our own hands. Rather, we place all things into divine hands and then act out of inner promptings.[44]

This same truth is brought out for us in Hebrews 4, where the writer reminds us that 'the promise of entering his rest still stands' (v. 1). He notes that Israel did not enter the promised land (where they would have found rest) because of their unbelief and disobedience. However, those who do believe and have faith can still enter into God's sabbath rest: 'There remains, then, a Sabbath-rest for the people of God; for anyone who enters God's rest also rests from his own work, just as God did from his' (vv. 9–10).

To rest in this sense means to live in the power of God rather than in our own energy and strength. It means that we depend on God to make things happen. We learn to receive from him all that we need to do his will. We depend upon the prior activity of God in our lives, and then respond in obedience. Andrew Murray, one of the greatest exponents of the inner life, comments on this verse:

> Entering the rest of God is the ceasing from self-effort and the yielding up of oneself in the full surrender of faith to God's working… As the Almighty, God is the only source of power. In nature he works all. In grace he waits to work all too, if man will but consent and allow. Truly to rest in God is to yield oneself up to the highest activity.[45]

Just as we love because he first loved us, so we work because he first moves within us. As we wait upon God, we expect him to create within us both the desire and ability to do his will (Philippians 2:13). We labour, but with all the energy that he inspires within us (Colossians 1:29). Being still before him is, therefore, an essential part in allowing his Spirit to work in us in this way.

From this perspective, faith gives rest because it rests in God, and it will mean ceasing from what has been called 'creaturely activity' – that is, the prideful expression of our independent self. Murray says, 'Faith is always repose in what Another will do for me. Faith ceases to seek help in itself or its own efforts, to be troubled with its need or its weakness; it rests in the sufficiency of the all-sufficient One who has undertaken all.'[46] For busy activists, being still for a while and letting go of our own activity may seem like a death, which indeed it is – a death to the old independent way of living, in order that the new life of the Spirit may be at work in us.

Resting in God does not mean resignation or idleness. What it means is that we are to work from a place of rest, not towards a place of rest. There is a world of difference between the two. Our ability to stop what we are doing and be still before God is an indicator of the direction in which our life is moving, and where the source of our strength really lies.

Watchman Nee, the great Chinese Christian writer, gives some helpful insights in his commentary on Ephesians. In seeking to explain what it means to be seated with Christ (Ephesians 2:6), he points out that after God had made the world in six days, he rested on the seventh. Adam was created on the sixth day, and so his first day was a day of rest. He began life with a day off! Nee describes it like this: 'Whereas God worked six days and then enjoyed his sabbath rest, Adam began his life with the sabbath; for God works before he rests, while man must first enter into God's rest, and then alone can he work.'[47]

According to Nee, this is the principle by which God always works. It was because God had finished his work of creation that Adam could begin by enjoying what God had already done for him. Likewise with our salvation: God has done everything for us in Christ on the cross. We simply step by faith into the enjoyment of his finished work. There is nothing for us to do: indeed, we must give up our own works in order to benefit from his. Watchman Nee writes:

> The first lesson we must learn is this, that the work is not initially ours at all, but his. It is not that we work for God, but that he works for us. God gives us our position of rest. He brings his Son's finished work and presents it to us, and then he says to us, 'Please sit' ... From this point onwards Christian experience proceeds as it began, not on the basis of our own work but always on that of the finished work of Another. Every new spiritual experience begins with the acceptance by faith of what God has done – with a new 'sitting down', if you like.[48]

To be seated with Christ, then, means to recognise our position in Christ and to realise that God has done everything for us in Christ, resting in the enjoyment and benefits of his work on our behalf. We allow him to take the strain and, just as we would entrust our whole weight to a chair, we entrust ourselves to him. Nee concludes, 'To sit down is simply to rest our whole weight – our load, ourselves, our future, everything – upon the Lord. We let him bear the responsibility and cease to carry it ourselves.'[49]

With this understanding firmly rooted within us of how God intends us to live, we can truly experience God's rest. Taking time out to be still and quiet before the Lord will become basic to the way we live and work, a joyful priority rather than a reluctant concession. We will be able to pace ourselves better, and will become more able to disentangle ourselves from extraneous demands. When the opportunity comes to sit and be still, we shall be able to do so in the knowledge that we are sitting down on the inside, too.

10

Silence

If we live in a busy world, we also live in a very noisy one. Activity and noise seem to go together, and they surround us. Those of us who are extraverts happily go along with this, getting a buzz from our involvement in the world out there, while others of a more introvert tendency learn to adapt to it, but long for more peace and quiet. Whatever our natural disposition, each of us needs sufficient space to ourselves so that our spirits can be renewed. One thing that all the great writers on the subject of the spiritual life stress is this: silence is indispensable to a deepening relationship with God. The question is how to be silent and find silence in a noisy world.

Even church is rarely quiet. A traditional evangelical church service is full of words. We sing words, pray words, read words and preach words – and then have the notices! Seldom is there any space to be still and listen to God. Many churches have little awareness of the power of silence or how to use it creatively within their worship.

Charismatic worship is very similar. Sometimes it feels as if the presence of the Spirit can only be measured in decibels, as music groups blast out the latest tunes and enthusiastic believers sing and clap their hearts out. Occasionally a gentler spirit prevails, but even then silence can be interpreted as a sign of non-involvement on the part of the congregation, or as if nothing is happening as far as God is concerned. Of course, the scriptures encourage us to praise God and to do so with enthusiasm; but we are also told that God is just as often present in the still, small voice (1 Kings 19:12–13; Psalm 46:10).

Many people are uncomfortable with silence. They do not know what to do with it, and do not appreciate its value. When there is a pause in the conversation or a gap in the flow of prayer, they may feel obliged to say or do something. They cannot rest in silence and always look for ways to cover it up with noise. This was certainly my own experience. I never knew what to do in times of silence, and found any interval for quietness both long and boring. The idea of a silent retreat was incomprehensible to me. However, since coming to understand the meaning and value of silence, I have begun to appreciate it increasingly and welcome it into my life.

Silence can be regarded as one of the main disciplines of the spiritual life.[50] The apostle James warns us clearly about the dangers of a careless tongue, and most of us know from first-hand experience what damage can be caused by careless words (James 3:1–12). Being able to control our words is therefore essential, and choosing to be silent is a mark of maturity. As Arsenius, one of the Desert Fathers, said, 'I have often repented of having spoken, but never of having been silent.'[51] A friend of mine loves to remind his associates, 'If you can't improve on the silence, don't say anything.'

There is obviously a time to speak out about injustice, inequality and so on, and, in that context, staying silent may be wrong, but the point I am making here is that our words have a way of running away with themselves and doing great damage. Words once spoken can seldom be taken back. We know that 'when words are many, sin is not absent', and that the person who holds his or her tongue is considered wise (Proverbs 10:19). By imposing on ourselves the discipline of not speaking, we begin the process of taming the tongue: 'The most frequent argument for silence is simply that words lead to sin. Not speaking, therefore, is the most obvious way to stay away from sin.'[52]

There is a time to speak and a time to be silent, and we need the discernment to know the difference. It is interesting to notice that, on some occasions, Jesus remained silent. When brought before his accusers, he refused to defend himself by justifying his actions

(Matthew 26:63). Richard Foster recognises that we often use words to manipulate situations and people and to adjust what others think of us. We are tempted to vindicate ourselves or retaliate. It requires great spiritual discipline to be silent and rest our case with God. Foster rightly says, 'One of the fruits of silence is the freedom to let our justification rest with God.'[53]

In developing a mature Christian character, one of our aims is therefore to learn when to speak and when to refrain from speaking (see Proverbs 25:11; Ecclesiastes 5:2). Only someone who is secure in God knows when it is right to say something and not be silent, and when it is better to remain silent and say nothing. The ability to be silent and listen to others is a skill that underpins many other important activities, especially in pastoral care and counselling. This is not just a matter of giving advice and offering our words of wisdom. Often, what people need most is simply a listening ear, and to be a good listener we must learn how to be silent ourselves.

Choosing to be silent is not a negative strategy. It has a positive aim. When we take time to be still and quiet before God, it is a way of opening ourselves up to him. In stillness we cease our activity; in silence we stop our talking. Both allow God the empty space in which he can draw near to us and begin a deeper work in our lives. Both silence and stillness are recreative, and merely sitting for a few moments without saying or doing anything will enrich us. Our souls will be fed and revitalised through the simple discipline of being quiet.

Silence can also be seen as our appropriate response to the presence of God. When God is present, the best thing for us to do is to remain silent. Consider these commands:

- 'The Lord is in his holy temple; let all the earth be silent before him' (Habakkuk 2:20).
- 'Be silent before the Sovereign Lord' (Zephaniah 1:7).
- 'Be still, and know that I am God' (Psalm 46:10).

Human words become inadequate and inappropriate when God draws near. There is a great temptation to say something, but we must beware of talking for the sake of it, as Peter did at the transfiguration, where it is said of him, 'He did not know what he was saying' (Luke 9:33). To interject human words at such a time is to tarnish the moment.

This was something I learned during a retreat with a group of fellow church leaders. We had begun a time of prayer and, as usual, I had started to pray for various situations in the church, trying as best as I could to come up with a solution for each problem and then ask God to act accordingly. In the midst of my prayer, I heard God say to me – as clearly as I have heard him say anything – 'Tony, please be quiet.' I knew in that instant that it would be wrong for me to continue praying as I had been doing. I shared briefly with the others what had happened, and we stopped our vocal prayer. Silence enveloped us and gripped us for the next 20 minutes. We were transfixed, hardly moving a muscle, unable to say anything. It was the most profound silence I have ever experienced. Words, especially human words, were totally out of place. It wasn't necessary to say or do anything: all that God required of us in that moment was simply to be, to rest before him. We knew he had already heard our prayers, that he had everything in hand. We simply basked in his love.

That morning, my understanding of silence was totally changed. I saw the difference between a God-given silence and an artificial, man-made silence. Our worship and prayer will bring us so far towards God, but there comes a moment when we have reached his presence (the Holy of Holies, as it were) and then the most appropriate thing for us to do is to kneel in silence before him. Once we have experienced such moments, we long for more. We cannot create them, however, or plan them into our services, for there is a 'givenness' about them. What we can do is to remain open to God, recognise when he is near and then respond accordingly.

The kind of prayer that I have just described is known as contemplative prayer. It is prayer without words. Contemplative prayer immerses us in the silence of God and, at its most basic, can be described as 'loving attentiveness to God'.[54] Alexander Ryrie explains it more fully:

> We are content simply to be with God, without inner words, and without requests, demands or expectations. With the silence of the spirit we cease to 'pray' in the usual sense of that word. Being still in the presence of God we acknowledge that our prayer comes not from ourselves but from God. In the prayer of silence it is God who prays within us, and we wait for him.[55]

Although making ourselves silent is a necessary preliminary to this form of prayer, at a deeper level it is really a matter of entering a silence that already exists. It has been said that 'silence' is one way of describing the being of God, and we often speak of 'the silence of eternity'. Certainly we can think of God as the still centre of the universe. Yes, God speaks to us and he uses words to do so, but words cannot convey all there is to know about him. To know him most fully, we need to embrace (or be embraced by) silence.

Within such silence, communion takes place. Communication is based on words, but communion is based on relationship. The closer we are to someone and the more confident we are with them, the more we can enjoy a companionable silence. This is the intimacy of lovers or the closest of friends. There is no need to ask anything, explain or impress. We can simply enjoy being together. This is the kind of communion that God seeks with us, which we can experience through his grace. It is the kind of spiritual intimacy illustrated in the Song of Songs, which exists between the Lover and the Beloved. When we are still and quiet, we create a space where God can draw near and embrace us in his love, and where we too can draw near to God and embrace him in our love.

Words are not necessary in communion, yet it is often in times of silence that God chooses to speak, and it is in such a context that we can most easily hear his voice: 'Though silence sometimes involves the absence of speech, it always involves the act of listening. Simply to refrain from talking, without a heart listening to God, is not silence.'[56]

What we 'hear' from God in the silence may not be actual words but rather a 'holy hunch' or an impression. In the stillness we may sense God's holiness, or know ourselves found, forgiven, restored, re-energised, equipped for service or simply loved. Even as God whispers words of love, affirmation and encouragement to us, maybe we find that we are given words that express more fully our love for him.

When we are still before God and attuned to his Spirit, we may also be given the words we need for others. We should pass these words on humbly, of course, with a cautious 'I think God may be saying this…', because any of us can be mistaken, and it is up to those receiving such words to recognise their authenticity. But words that are born out of silence have greater power than those that flow freely and easily, but without much depth. Our words can take on a prophetic edge simply because we have been still in God's presence and listened to him. In this sense, silence teaches us to speak: 'A word with power is a word that comes out of silence.'[57] Perhaps this is what the prophet Isaiah meant when he spoke about having an 'instructed tongue'. He recognised that God was able to place in his heart and mind encouraging words to pass on to others. The important thing for him was to listen attentively to what God might be saying to him (see Isaiah 50:4).

At the same time, contemplative prayer has value, whether or not we think we hear God speaking to us. It is enough for us to feel that we are in God's presence, whether or not we receive anything from him. Indeed, those schooled in contemplative prayer would suggest that it is sufficient for us to be still before God, and that we should not seek any feedback or feeling of 'getting somewhere' or hearing the voice of God. This cuts right across the charismatic desire for direct experience of God, with specific content and immediate significance, and may therefore be one of the most difficult aspects of contemplative prayer for some of us to grasp.

Henri Nouwen, with his long experience of teaching people how to develop the inner life, strongly encouraged the practice of silence. He suggested that ours is a culture of too many words, both spoken and written, in which the greatest danger for ministers is the temptation towards too many words. According to Nouwen, silence protects the spiritual fire within, and we must guard it by not speaking too much and thereby cheapening our words: 'Silence guards the inner heat of religious emotions. The inner heat is the life of the Holy Spirit within us. Thus silence is the discipline by which the inner fire of God is tended and kept alive.'[58]

When we are so used to sharing with others what God is doing in our life, this advice may seem surprising, but there is wisdom in it. Sometimes we need to take time to meditate on what God is saying and doing in our lives, so that we fully understand it ourselves, and sometimes it is better to hold on to a word from God until the time is right to share it. We can dissipate the power and presence of God in our life by being too quick with our words. Silence enables us to reflect on the events of life and derive spiritual meaning from them. Like Mary at the birth of Jesus, we need to treasure up some things in our hearts and ponder them at our leisure (Luke 2:19).

Perhaps now it is easier to see why silence is so indispensable to the growth and development of our spiritual lives. Silence moves us away from the surface of life into the deeper reaches of the heart and the spirit. It opens us up to the movement of God by his Spirit: 'Now to tread the spiritual path we must learn to be silent. What is required of us is a journey into profound silence.'[59]

As I write this, I am reminded of my first experience of a silent retreat. I had arranged to spend time with David and Joyce Huggett at their lovely home in Derbyshire. Although I would meet with one of them on a daily basis, most of the time would be spent alone and in silence. The retreat had been planned for several months, but, when the time came, I found myself not wanting to go. If I could have found an honourable way out, I would have taken it.

As I packed beforehand, I remember thinking to myself, 'This is not a good idea!' There was so much work to do and I felt guilty about leaving it all behind. Furthermore, it had not been a good time for me spiritually. I hardly felt in the mood for a retreat. My emotions were all over the place and I could only see myself getting even more depressed if I were left alone. My normal way of coping with stress is to be with other people, not on my own. I wondered how I would manage, being cut off from my family, with no television or newspapers and none of my favourite reading material. As I set off, it felt as if I was going into exile. I consoled myself by thinking that I could always leave early if I didn't like it.

Joyce greeted me on arrival, and her warm, accepting smile told me I was very welcome. Something inside me said, 'Maybe it won't be so bad after all.' After settling in and attending a brief chapel service, I was left to my own devices for the first part of the evening. I sat and relaxed in the sitting-room, its windows overlooking the beautiful Derbyshire hills.

There was silence all around me. In the stillness, something totally unexpected happened to me. I felt God come to me, and his presence rest upon me. It was completely out of the blue as far as I was concerned, and absolutely unmerited. It was a special gift from God the Father to one of his very needy children. It marked the beginning of three days of wonderful intimacy with God, made all the more special because it was so unexpected and so undeserved. I could not believe the transformation that took place inside me.

I wrote in my journal, 'If you can't come to the silence, let the silence come to you. It has a way of creeping in, of creeping up on you. In a silent place you begin to feel quiet inside. Even if you arrive agitated, let the silence come to you.'

The retreat was a turning-point for me. From that time onwards, I discovered the value of silence and what can happen when we learn to befriend it. It opened a doorway for me into another, deeper realm of Christian experience.

11

Solitude

Stillness and silence thrive best in a context of solitude. In other words, if I am to be truly still and able to wait silently before God, I will need at some point to spend time alone.

Of course we can seek God in the company of others – indeed, there is a corporate dimension to knowing God – but, in order to develop my own inner life fully, I need to withdraw for a while from other people and the normal routine, so that I can meet with God at a more intimate level. David Runcorn notes, 'The call to solitude is the call to centre our lives deeply and radically in the heart of God alone. It is not a rejection of activity or busyness as such. Solitude will give our lives a firm foundation.'[60]

Throughout history, people have always sought communion with God in quiet and solitary places. They have responded to the call to get away from others in order to spend time with him. In the lands of the Bible, the desert provided an ideal place to be alone. Jesus often withdrew to such lonely places, and we could also think of Moses and Elijah, whose ministries involved time in the desert. John the Baptist was shaped by the wilderness, and the apostle Paul spent three years in the wastelands of Arabia as he came to grips with what God was doing in his life.

The Desert Fathers, in the early centuries of the Church's existence, deliberately went into the wilderness for solitary prayer and silence. There they sought God and engaged the powers of darkness. They developed profound insights into the ways of God and became famed for their wisdom. Even today, their teachings inspire those who look for spiritual wisdom and guidance.[61] Likewise, the continuing existence of monastic orders bears witness to the understanding that aloneness is an integral part of the spiritual life. They particularly value solitude within the context of community. Within their traditions they hold a rich heritage of Christian truth and wisdom, often overlooked by evangelicals but from which we can certainly profit.

Some people enjoy their own company, and the idea of solitariness holds no fears for them. Others of us are more gregarious and prefer people around us. The prospect of time alone (even with God) fills us not with excitement but, rather, with apprehension.

Without realising it, many of us are uncomfortable with ourselves, which is why we do not enjoy being alone. Our noise and activity are all part of our defence systems. Once these are removed and we are alone before God, we can feel terribly exposed and needy. It is this inner anxiety that God wants to touch and heal. Rather than looking to meet it through other people and endless activities, we begin to realise that it can only be met fully in God himself. Solitude is part of the process by which we develop a greater attachment to God and a less possessive hold on people or the diversions that life offers. As one prayer puts it, 'Show me how to approach my sense of being alone and cut off, so that it may not be any longer a condition to be dreaded, but rather seen as a means to closer dependence upon you. Let my soul learn in solitude the lesson of your presence.'[62]

Chosen times of solitude, therefore, have a way of refining us. They contain what the Quaker tradition calls the 'sifting silence', disturbing to experience but the kind of clearing-out of our spiritual systems that God requires. It has been called 'solitary refinement'! As we experience it, we may find that hidden issues begin to surface within us – buried resentments, old wounds, long-forgotten hurts, missed opportunities. We may begin to see our own twisted motives and, in retrospect, feel regret over some of our actions and attitudes. Issues we thought were resolved long ago may reappear with renewed energy. It may well feel as if God has taken the lid off the hidden places of our hearts.

Janice had always had a difficult relationship with her father. A solitary man, he was uncommunicative and rarely expressed affection. Janice felt rejected and a deep resentment built up inside her. Her father was also harsh towards her mother, and Janice often found herself defending her mother from his verbal attacks. After she became a Christian, Janice sought a better relationship with her father. Tearfully, she apologised for her attitude towards him. He made no response, gave no reply and didn't even acknowledge her presence.

Janice did everything in her power to put things right. She repented of her resentment and, as best she could, forgave him. She received prayer for her own inner hurts. However, she still felt a continuing need to talk about her father and to blame him for his behaviour. Then, some ten years after he had died, God stepped in.

Janice was spending time alone. Her house overlooked some beautiful Scottish hills and, as she drank in the splendour, she began to pray. As she prayed, she began to cry. She cried and cried, as God began to heal the hurts inside her and set her free from the constant need to criticise her father. God did for her in solitude what she could not do for herself. She was transformed through the silence. Today she can talk freely about her father and acknowledge his weakness without any trace of bitterness or the need to condemn him.

Henri Nouwen regarded this kind of experience as one of the main blessings of solitude. For him, solitude was the furnace of transformation, where God takes away the false scaffolding that surrounds our lives and strips us of our unhelpful dependencies. Solitude is not primarily a place for privacy or even rest and renewal: 'Rather, it is the place of conversion, the place where the old self dies and the new self is born, the place where the emergence of the new man and the new woman occurs.'[63]

Nouwen particularly encouraged ministers to free themselves from the 'compulsions' of ministry (the temptation to be relevant, spectacular and powerful) and to face up to their own 'nothingness'. Only then could the struggle with self give way to the transforming encounter with Jesus that leads to fruitful ministry.

Scripture tells us that the sight of God (and the blessing that accompanies it) is reserved for the pure in heart (Matthew 5:8), and we should not be at all surprised if a deep cleansing work accompanies a determined desire to know God better. Repentance is always met with forgiving grace:

> When we are willing to wait in solitude and silent prayer before God, the Holy Spirit begins to recentre our lives, picking through all the distracted fragments and confusion, to the heart of who we are, to the place where God's love waits to welcome us. There we wait in hope and longing for the unfolding of the great secret, kept in God's love – the secret of who we are, in the image of the One who created us.[64]

This recentring of our lives is one of the basic and central aspects of the spiritual life. Our search for God includes the search for ourselves. The two cannot be disentangled. In finding him, we find ourselves; in knowing him, we know ourselves. We know and are known (Galatians 4:9). There is a deep place within each of us, which the Bible calls the 'heart', and it is the heart that longs for God. As Richard Foster says, 'Perhaps somewhere in the subterranean chambers of your life you have heard the call to deeper, fuller living. Perhaps you have become weary of frothy experiences and shallow teaching. Every now and then you have caught the glimpses, hints of something more than you have known. Inwardly, you have longed to launch out into the deep.'[65]

While, for some people, solitude may well lead to experiences of spiritual intimacy, even ecstasy, not everyone has such experiences and they should not become an end in themselves. Sometimes, because of the nature of God's work within us, we may find ourselves void of feelings, experiencing what was described by St John of the Cross, a 16th-century Spanish contemplative, as 'the dark night of the soul'.[66] During such times, God has to be known as much in his perceived absence as in his presence. Paradoxically, presence and absence go together. Much as we would like to experience good feelings all the time, they are the gift of God and cannot be manufactured by our own efforts. Fundamentally, God, and the ways of God, remain a mystery, never under our control.

For Andrew, an active member of a charismatic church, this was how he discovered the value of contemplative prayer. He had experienced for the first time a long period of spiritual darkness, which he found difficult to understand. It was his inability to pray using words during this time, and the sense of the absence of God, that led him to make a deliberate choice to pray without words. With the help of a spiritual director, he began to realise that the 'dark night of the soul' was, in fact, quite normal, not a sign that he had somehow 'backslidden'. This came as an enormous relief to him, for within his evangelical background he had no framework to understand such an experience.

Evangelicals and charismatics often feel guilty if they are not experiencing God and hearing his voice all the time, with little understanding of what to do when this doesn't happen. Many worry that they are failing in their walk with God, when, in fact, God is entrusting them with the opportunity to deepen their faith and trust him even when there are no tangible signs of his presence.

Times of regular solitude are essential to effective ministry. Henri Nouwen went as far as to say that real ministry flows out of solitude, for ministry can and must be the result of direct and intimate encounter with Jesus. In solitude, ministry and spirituality meet each other. As we still ourselves to encounter God and allow him to transform us, compassion is born into our hearts. We can feel the pain of others because we have felt our own pain. We can understand their brokenness because we have encountered our own. Those who have been forgiven much love much. As Nouwen wrote, 'What becomes visible here is that solitude moulds self-righteous people into gentle, caring, forgiving persons who are so deeply convinced of their own great sinfulness and so fully aware of God's even greater mercy that their life itself becomes ministry.'[67] In solitude we do not move away from people. Instead, our hearts draw closer to them. We learn to identify ourselves with them and with the whole world.

How do we find this solitude? Sometimes it is not so much chosen as given. The circumstances of life may cause us to be isolated, cut off and alone. Even though we may not welcome such events, they provide a wonderful opportunity for us to learn solitude.

Audrey had been working for the British Embassy in Cambodia. It was a period of intense activity for her, both in her working life and at home. When the opportunity came for a holiday in the UK, the family could hardly wait. However, within ten days of arriving home, Audrey was struck down with a violent attack of dengue fever (a form of malaria). One day, as she was lying in bed, too weak to do anything else, God spoke to her: 'Is this what I have to do to get you to be still and listen to me?' Audrey was shocked. She had thought that by being the good 'all-round mum', she was doing what God wanted. But no, God was right. Somewhere in her busyness, and in looking out for and organising everyone else, she had lost the peaceful place in the middle of her heart that belonged to God.

Slowly, as she started to recover, she began to read *Open to God* by Joyce Huggett.[68] As she read, a small revolution took place within her. She began to realise that it was more than permissible to stop and listen to God: it was essential. She began to learn a 'new' kind of prayer, contemplative prayer, whereby she was content to wait before God in silence. Gradually she regained her perspective and excitement at knowing the living God. This became a defining moment in her Christian life. When she returned to Cambodia some weeks later, she was full of joy and enthusiasm because of all that God had done for her.

At other times, solitude is a choice, and we must make our own space. It may come in the little intervals of our day that provide us with aloneness; it may be through the regular daily discipline of time spent with God; it may be by means of a planned withdrawal for a retreat or quiet day. In carving out time to be alone, we are not being selfish, for this is how we will maintain our ability to serve those in need. It is not a luxury, for, if we do not look after ourselves, eventually we will no longer be able to care for others. Solitude is essential, and it will refresh and renew us, sharpen our ability to hear the voice of God and help us discern his purposes for our lives.

Ruth Hayley Barton has said that 'the longing for solitude is the longing for God'.[69] If she is right, and I believe she is, then it is vital that we fashion our own 'piece of desert' and make it a meeting place with God. The very thirsting of our souls is the divine invitation to intimacy, and we should respond gladly and willingly.

Keep company with me

Having responded to the invitation of Jesus to be with him, we now consider how to develop our friendship with him. What will take us deeper in our relationship with him? What will help us to know him more fully? Here we look at three of the disciplines of grace – practical means by which the life of Christ can be imparted to us. They are reflection, Bible meditation and contemplation. We are called to think carefully about our lives and how we live, to consider well what God is saying to us in scripture and creation, and to dwell in his presence, gazing upon him and drinking in his beauty. Once again there is a measure of overlap between the three disciplines but sufficient distinctiveness for us to consider them individually.

12

Reflection

We were nearing the end of a time of prayer in our home group and had reached the point where we felt comfortable to sit in silence for a moment or two. The house was unusually quiet. As we sat in the stillness, the only sound we could hear was the clock above the fireplace. Tick, tock, tick, tock. So rhythmic, and so faithful in its routine. It occurred to me that most days, no one in that house would notice the clock, although it was always ticking away reliably. Its sound would be drowned out by the everyday noise of normal family living. But in this moment, because we were stilled, we were able to hear its sound.

God is always speaking to us. Faithfully, day by day, his word goes forth. Often, because of our busyness, we do not hear what he is saying to us. Only when we still ourselves can we hear his quiet, gentle, insistent whisper. Reflection is one of the means by which we teach ourselves to hear the word that is all around us.

The ability to reflect is the ability to 'think backwards'. In the mental process of reflection, we are able to recall events and consider their significance, to recognise what is happening in our lives. As we take time to think over things, we can evaluate them, enjoying again the positive aspects and learning from our mistakes so that their impact is not lost. It is easy to see why reflection is an integral part of developing the inner life.

When Jesus commanded his disciples to remember him through the breaking of bread (Communion or Eucharist), he was encouraging them to make the discipline of reflection part of their normal life. He was suggesting that they regularly pause in their routine in order to think back over the events of his death, so that they would not lose the significance of what he had done for them.

Later, the apostle Paul suggested another reflective activity in preparation for the breaking of bread – that of examining ourselves before partaking. Taking time to think over our life and behaviour is a safeguard against eating and drinking unworthily (1 Corinthians 11:28). It is a discipline that needs to be cultivated in a world where we dash from one activity to another, with little or no thought for the significance of what we are doing. Self-examination need not be a negative exercise. It is as much about recognising what we have done right as about what we may have done wrong; and, in the context of God's unconditional and unchanging love for us, we dare to face up to our shortcomings because we know that forgiveness and acceptance are available. Only thus can we be transformed and grow in Christian character. 'Examine yourselves,' Paul tells the wayward Corinthians, 'to see whether you are in the faith; test yourselves. Do you not realise that Christ Jesus is in you – unless, of course, you fail the test?' (2 Corinthians 13:5).

Throughout the Old Testament, we see that the Jews were also encouraged to 'remember' what God had done for them, especially in bringing them out of slavery in Egypt. By stopping and reflecting on where they had come from and on the mighty acts of God, they would be protected from the ever-present danger of wandering away from the Lord: 'Remember how the Lord your God led you all the way in the desert these forty years, to humble you and to test you in order to know what was in your heart, whether or not you would keep his commands' (Deuteronomy 8:2; see vv. 1–20). By consciously looking back and considering their history, their love would be rekindled, their faith strengthened and their understanding of God's ways increased.

The prophets also called Israel to be a reflective people in order to avoid the spiritual apathy that so often dogged their progress.

Haggai, for instance, rallied the people of his day who had largely ignored the interests of God in favour of their own concerns, with this call: 'Give careful thought to your ways' (1:5, 7). Only by reflecting on their lives would they be able to recognise how far they had slipped away from God. Likewise, after they have rebuilt the foundation of the temple, the prophet calls on them not to lose the significance of the event: 'From this day on... give careful thought to the day when the foundation of the Lord's temple was laid. Give careful thought' (2:18). Experience was to be their teacher, but they would learn the lessons only if they reflected on what had happened. By giving careful consideration to all that had taken place, they would be able to learn from their mistakes and ultimately to profit from them. Often we fail to learn the lessons God has for us simply because we do not take time to reflect.

Spiritual truth is absorbed largely through the process of reflection. Not only do we need to hear the truth, but we must take time to think it over and consider its implications for our lives. So Paul exhorts Timothy, 'Reflect on what I am saying, for the Lord will give you insight into all this' (2 Timothy 2:7).

Here we see the biblical way to spiritual understanding. As we humbly reflect in our minds, the Holy Spirit grants revelation in our hearts. The two processes go together and are inseparable. We do not arrive at spiritual understanding through our own ability. We are dependent upon revelation from God, who rarely grants such revelation in a vacuum. He gives it to those who take time to sit and think about his word. As John Stott comments, 'For the understanding of Scripture a balanced combination of thought and prayer is essential. We must do the considering, and the Lord will do the giving of understanding.'[70]

One contemporary author who has brought to our attention again the importance of reflection is the American writer Ken Gire. Through his books *The Reflective Life* and *Windows of the Soul*, he urges us to adopt a more reflective approach to living, so that we may hear more clearly the voice of God. God's word is all around us – in our life events, in scripture, in books, in the theatre or cinema, in countless ordinary places – if we would but recognise it. Gire writes, 'The reflective life is a life that is attentive, receptive, and responsive to what God is doing in us and around us. It's a life that asks God to reach into our heart, allowing him to touch us there, regardless of the pleasure it excites or the pain it inflicts.'[71]

The reflective life makes us aware of the sacredness that surrounds us, which often we do not see. In order to live more reflectively, we need to slow down. To benefit fully from what God is saying to us or doing in our lives, we need to stop and pause. Only then will we recognise and respond to those God-given moments that come to each of us: 'Living reflectively provides opportunities during our day for a closer look at things, at people, at ourselves, and at God. The faster the pace of life, though, the more we will miss those opportunities.'[72] By slowing down, we are able to see what is sacred and recognise the presence and activity of God in the ordinariness of our own lives.

On one retreat I attended, we were asked to do an 'awareness walk'. We were encouraged to walk in the grounds of the house where we were staying and use our senses to encounter God. The retreat leader suggested that we look carefully and in detail at what was around us, noticing things we might otherwise miss, listening to the sounds we may not normally hear and 'feeling' what was there in the garden.

It was a crisp autumn morning. I was surprised at how readily God spoke to me and how easy it became to pray. I came across a shrub with some colourful berries, the kind that birds love to eat in winter. It reminded me how God provides for them (and us), and how the birds scatter the tiny seeds, causing other plants to grow elsewhere. I thought of Christians being scattered by circumstances and taking the gospel with them, and prayed for the spread of the Church throughout the world.

Further on, I picked up an apple, lying neglected on the ground along with dozens of others that had never been harvested. It made me think of those who had never had the chance to hear the gospel. I prayed that the Lord of the harvest would send labourers into the harvest field, that the fruit would not be lost (Luke 10:2; John 4:35).

At the bottom of the garden, a holly bush was covered in bright red berries, reminding me of Christmas. I thought of my sister, who had sung 'The holly and the ivy' in church as a girl, and prayed for her. I thought too of the Saviour who had shed his blood for each of us, so that there might be a gospel to preach.

With very little effort on my part, I had enjoyed a time of rich communion with God, simply because I had been encouraged to slow down, notice what was around me and listen for the voice of God. Nature is full of parables, if only we become aware of what is there and cultivate a heightened sense of awareness that God may have something to say in whatever grabs our attention.

Gire speaks of three 'habits of the heart', which help us to nurture a reflective life and heighten our awareness of the sacred:

- Reading the moment: using our eyes to see what is on the surface, actually noticing what is going on around us.
- Reflecting on the moment: engaging our mind to look beneath the surface and consider its significance.
- Responding to the moment: allowing what we have seen or felt to have a place in our heart, and allowing it to grow there, upward to God and outward towards other people.

Using these three simple steps, we can benefit from any God-given moment that occurs in our life, whether it be a chance conversation with another person, something that catches our attention in a book, or a scene in a film that speaks to us. God is continually planting the seeds of his word into our life, in countless different ways every day. By recognising such moments, reflecting on them and responding to them, we can capture those heavenly seeds. Something of eternal significance can then be planted within us.

Journalling

One of the most helpful and practical ways of learning to reflect is to use a journal. By writing down and recording the things that happen to us, along with our feelings and responses, we are able to reflect honestly about ourselves and begin to trace God's hand at work in our lives. Gire notes:

> [Journalling] helps us see what we look at. When we journal, it's like taking a Polaroid of some moment during the day that has caught our attention. Only we do it with words instead of with film. But like that film, what we have looked at often develops right before our very eyes as we're writing, revealing things we hadn't seen before.[73]

Christians down the centuries have benefited from journalling, and it is regarded as one of the classic spiritual disciplines. A journal is more than a diary, for its purpose is to record not merely events but the significance of those events. It is a personal record of what is happening inside us and, therefore, focuses on our thoughts and feelings. Its purpose is to help us understand ourselves and recognise the activity and voice of God in our lives. Writer Richard Peace says that journalling helps us pay attention to God and is a way of hearing and responding to God. He notes, 'For those who seek to follow Jesus, journals are an ideal way to track their journey and to interact with Jesus along the way. Journals help them to know themselves and God, and to see God at work in the intricacies of their lives.'[74]

Journals can be used for many purposes but they have particular relevance for spiritual growth. We can use them to record our thoughts and insights during Bible study, or to note things that puzzle or interest us. We can use them as a prayer diary, recording our requests and noting the outcomes. We can be very honest, confessing our sins, identifying the issues we are struggling with and trying to understand them better as we write. We can 'think as we write', meditating on our lives and actions, looking back over what has happened and evaluating it. A journal is a wonderful tool to help us get in touch with our real selves and our innermost thoughts. It is a safe place, where we can learn to be real and authentic. A journal, well used, will become a trusted friend.

Why is it so helpful to journal in this way? Because the very act of writing down what we are thinking (if we are willing to be honest) is liberating in itself. As we write, our thoughts are clarified, perspective is gained and insight develops. Things we were afraid of become less threatening when written down. Issues that were confused become clearer. Instead of possibly deceiving ourselves, we are enabled to get in touch with our real selves and face up to things as they really are. Writing allows us to get in touch with feelings that might otherwise be unhealthily repressed or buried away. Journalling enables us to explore these emotions and express them in an appropriate and safe way. Dreams, which are often a clue to what is going on in our inner lives, can also be recorded and reflected on.[75]

Through reflective writing, we enter into a dialogue with God. Our writing is a conversation with him and, not surprisingly, he often has something to say. In the very act of expressing ourselves, openly and honestly, we often hear God speak a word of guidance, reassurance, understanding or acceptance. Communication is at the heart of our relationship with God, and journalling is an aid to both talking and listening to God. When placed within the wider context of being alone with God, journalling becomes not only a way to understand ourselves better but also to love ourselves better. Whatever we discover about ourselves, we do so in the knowledge that God loves us unconditionally. We need not be afraid to express ourselves freely when we have the safety net of God's grace beneath us.

Over a period of time, journals become a record of our spiritual journey, showing where we have come from, where we are and pointing us to where we may be going. They become a rich source of inspiration to us as we chart the way God has led us, answered our prayers and made provision for us. They become our personal book of Psalms.

Richard Peace suggests that we can use journalling for other specific purposes, especially in understanding our life history and coming to terms with the past, as well as in thinking about the future and discerning God's will. He writes, 'Journalling helps us understand our unfolding story. Knowing our story helps us see what God has been doing in the past, is doing now, and is calling us to do in the future.'[76]

One of my friends, Greg, has benefited enormously from journalling. Not by nature a reflective person, he was introduced to the idea by his mentor. He tried it and was amazed by how helpful he found it, especially in working through some of his more negative emotions. Now journalling has become part of his daily routine. First thing in the morning, while the house is still quiet and the children asleep, Greg is at work on his journal. Not only does he reflect on how he is feeling, but he notes what he feels God is saying to him and keeps a record of helpful things he has read. Every now and then, he looks back over what he has written to see any trends or patterns and to be reminded of important things that have happened.

Socrates famously said that the unexamined life is not worth living. Lives that are busy and always on the move do have a tendency to be shallow and scattered. Those who wish for something more substantial, for something deeper and more focused, must give themselves the time and space to reflect.

13

Bible meditation (*lectio divina*)

Anyone can meditate. When Isaac went out into the field in the early evening to meditate (Genesis 24:63), he was doing what many of us do instinctively: he was taking a moment to be still and think his own thoughts. He deliberately chose a quiet time of the day when he could be relaxed, and a familiar and lonely place where he would be undisturbed. There, in the tranquillity of the evening, he was free to gather his thoughts. All of us need such recreating moments in our lives, when we can bring our fragmented selves to order. This is the heart of meditation.

If reflection is about 'thinking backwards', meditation is about 'thinking deeply'. When we meditate, we take time to think through issues, to look at them first this way and then that way. We chew things over in our minds as a cow chews the cud – going over and over until our thoughts become clear and settled.

Worry is a form of meditation. When we worry about something, we continually dwell on something negative and unhelpful. We allow our imagination to run wild, thinking of all the bad things that might happen. So we are meditating, but unhealthily. This shows that we can all meditate. It is not a matter of intelligence or spiritual prowess. What is important, though, is that we meditate in the right way. We can choose what we meditate upon, and it is possible, with discipline and practice, to turn our minds to more uplifting thoughts.

This is what Mary did at the birth of Jesus. So many wonderful things happened to her in such a short space of time that she couldn't take them all in at once. Rather, she stored them up in her heart and, over a period of time, dwelt on them for herself, thinking through the significance of what had taken place: 'But Mary treasured up all these things and pondered them in her heart' (Luke 2:19). In this way, Mary's faith was built up and she was strengthened within herself. Meditation is one of the main ways by which we can go deeper in spiritual matters. It takes us from the merely superficial into a consideration of more substantial matters. This is why it is regarded as a central part of Christian devotion and a key aspect of contemplative spirituality.

One of the Hebrew words used in the Old Testament for 'meditation' (*hagah*) suggests a muttering or speaking quietly to oneself. It seems that meditating in ancient Israel involved repeating or murmuring key texts in a low voice, reciting God's word to oneself. This form of meditation was popular with the Desert Fathers, who made the words of scripture their own by memorising them and repeating them over and over again with profound concentration. In this way, the term 'meditation' has come to refer to the use of short repeated prayers, spoken quietly over and over again. The Jesus Prayer ('Lord Jesus Christ, Son of God, have mercy on me'), which I have mentioned already, is one of the most widely used. Typically, such a prayer calls on God to be present and have mercy or grant help. It is repeated constantly along with the rhythm of the breathing. As well as helping to reduce distractions, this method of prayer becomes a way for moving the attention from the head to the heart. Alexander Ryrie comments, 'Through this kind of prayer one is taken out of one's thoughts and led into the deepest and most central part of oneself, the heart, the secret, inmost place which no one else can enter, the place where one is most truly oneself.'[77]

Such 'prayers of the heart' lead us deeper into God. For many people, they become the means of praying continually and open up a stream of prayer for those who practise this form of meditation diligently.

The other word for meditation in the Old Testament is *suach*, and this describes silent, inward thinking, pondering or reflecting. This kind of meditation usually has an object and, most commonly, is focused upon the word of God. Christian meditation is distinctive in that it is primarily centred on the revelation of God through the Bible.

Meditating on scripture is different from Bible study. In Bible study, we seek to analyse a passage and understand it intellectually. When we meditate on scripture, we take just a small portion and seek to internalise it, making the meaning personal and looking for the impact it can have in our lives. We are seeking to allow the word of God to sink down from our heads to our hearts, to transform and change us. We are listening to what God has to say to us today as individuals, rather than what he has to say in general to all people at all times.

Thus, with the help of the Holy Spirit, we might take a verse or phrase of scripture and mull it over in our minds, asking the Spirit to give us understanding and revelation. All the time, we are seeking to apply the truths we discover to our own lives, honestly responding in obedience to what we find there. We are not looking for something to share with others but for what God has to say to us personally.

Joyce Huggett explains the purpose:

> We meditate to give God's words the opportunity to penetrate, not just our minds, but our emotions – the places where we hurt – and our will – the place where we make our choices and decisions. We meditate to encounter the Living Word, Jesus himself. We meditate so that every part of our being, our thoughts and our affections and our ambitions, are turned to face and honour and glorify him.[78]

We can see from this that Christian meditation is different from other forms of meditation, such as those associated with Eastern religions. Rather than emptying the mind, Christian meditation is about filling the mind with the word of God; and rather than being about 'detachment' from everything around us, it is more about 'attachment', seeking to be joined more closely to Christ and his word. Peter Toon, in his book *Meditating as a Christian*, makes this distinction very clear, and even suggests that 'formative reading' may be a better term to use, since the purpose of Christian meditation is to be 'formed' or shaped by the text of scripture. He writes:

> I do not hold the Bible in my hand in order to analyse, dissect or to gather information from it. Rather I hold it in order to let my Master penetrate the depths of my being with his Word and thus facilitate inner moral and spiritual transformation. I am there in utter dependence upon our God – who is the Father to whom I pray, the Son through whom I pray, and the Holy Spirit in whom I pray.[79]

The aim of meditation is to meet with Jesus, the Beloved One. We read the scriptures as a love letter and approach them carefully and tenderly, savouring each word so that we can find him. Toon continues:

> We perhaps need constantly to remind ourselves that the end and aim of formative reading is to seek Christ in the inspired and sacred text in order to discover the love of God, to savour that love and to be united in faith and love with the Bridegroom of our souls. My soul may be compared to the honey bee who gathers from the sweet, spiritual flowers of God's revelation the divine pollen in order to taste the heavenly sweetness of the salvation which is in Jesus.[80]

Many devotional writers point out the importance of using the imagination when meditating upon the scriptures. This was particularly the recommendation of Ignatius of Loyola in his Spiritual Exercises. He encouraged his followers to visualise the gospels. Richard Foster also encourages this approach, feeling that 'the inner world of meditation is most easily entered through the door of the imagination'.[81] Few people, he suggests, can approach meditation in a purely abstract way. Thus, when we meditate on the scriptures, we should seek to take our place within the story and to use our senses to imagine what it was like. By feeling the story, we can enter into the text and the text can enter into us.

For example, take the story of Jesus washing the feet of the disciples (John 13:2–17). Try to visualise the scene in the upper room in your mind, with the smell of the meal being prepared in the background and the buzz of conversation. Use your senses to help you recreate the scene and imagine yourself being there, perhaps as one of the disciples. What does it feel like to be there? Is there an embarrassing silence when Jesus takes the towel and the bowl and acts as a servant? How do you respond when he comes to you and washes your feet? What might you say to him, and he to you? What is the overall impact of the story upon you?

This is an approach with which theologian Alister McGrath is in full agreement. In his book *The Journey*, he describes his own discovery of the practice of biblical meditation. He says that Western Christianity, influenced by the 18th-century Enlightenment and its emphasis on reason, has neglected the imagination and the emotions. As he began to meditate on scripture, he found that as well as understanding biblical truth, he was able to appreciate it. McGrath began to explore the theme of projecting oneself into scripture and allowing oneself to be caught up in the story. He says:

> I had to think of myself as being there, witnessing what was said and done. I began to read the gospel narratives with new excitement... Meditating in this way on the gospel text led naturally to an enhanced appreciation of all that Jesus is, and all that he has done for me. It led most naturally into prayer. Reading the Bible leads to meditating on the Bible which leads to praying from the Bible.[82]

While the scriptures are the main source of material for meditation, they themselves encourage us to broaden our outlook and find God everywhere around us. This is especially so in creation, for God has inscribed many of his most important lessons in the world of nature. Jesus often found spiritual meaning and insight from the everyday things around him, and drew the attention of his disciples to what was right before their very eyes. 'Look at the birds,' he said. 'Consider the lilies. Think about the grass of the field' (see Matthew 6:25–34).

Sister Margaret Magdalen suggests that these simple things were to be the icons (spiritual pictures) through which the disciples would penetrate the mystery of God's providence and protection, and discover hidden wisdom and truth about God's relationship with his creation. She says, 'The disciples are invited to consider, to notice, to learn from the lilies, not by peremptory glance but by a long, feasting look. "Consider" has about it the feeling of restful reflection, leisurely appreciation, a freedom of heart to gaze and wonder, and, in doing so, to discover truth.'[83]

Life today, with its constant rushing, leaves little time for this kind of meditation. There is so little opportunity to stop and stare, for 'walking and gawking' (to use one of Joyce Huggett's favourite expressions). We are poorer as a result. Spiritual wisdom often remains hidden from view, yet it is all around us: 'Go to the ant, you sluggard; consider its ways and be wise' (Proverbs 6:6). Who would have thought that a simple creature like the ant could teach us anything? Yet a careful observation of its ways, a willingness to sit and to study, to watch and reflect, reveals one of the most profound lessons of life – that nothing is achieved without hard work and that diligence is a quality to be sought after, both in spiritual matters and life in general. It is not only the ant that can teach us wisdom: every creature, every bird, every plant, every tree or flower, has its own insights to impart to those with eyes to see.

I was watching some squirrels scampering through the trees one day. I marvelled at their agility and their ability to know which branches would bear their weight. These were well-built squirrels who obviously had a large store of nuts somewhere. As they darted here and there, they were so skilful in making their way through the branches and the multiplicity of options available to them. Whether they went up, down, left or right didn't seem to matter to them, as long as they were heading generally in the right direction.

It spoke to me about guidance. Sometimes we feel paralysed by the many choices before us; we are fearful of choosing the wrong option and making a mistake. But if we prayerfully commit our way to God and seek his wisdom, he is able to bring us to the best place for us to be. If we take what feels like a wrong turning, he can always lead us by another way.

Nor should we forget the overall impact that creation can have upon us. As we stand before the majesty of mountains and oceans, deserts and forests, we begin to feel our own smallness. We begin to bring our lives into perspective, to feel a true estimate of our own humanity and finiteness. Such moments encourage in us a sense of humility, of knowing our place within the universe. As the psalmist wrote, 'When I consider your heavens, the work of your fingers, the moon and the stars, which you have set in place, what is man that you are mindful of him, the son of man that you care for him?' (Psalm 8:3–4).

We need to recapture this sense of wonder if it is missing from our lives. We can become so preoccupied with ourselves and our concerns that we lose our sense of proportion. Getting out into the broad open spaces, alone with God in his creation, can have a profoundly restorative effect on us, especially if we allow ourselves to pause, and think, and reflect.

We can meditate on anything that points us towards God. We can even meditate on the injustice and pain in the world and ponder the mysteries of human existence. We can meditate on the events of our time and seek to understand their significance, looking to God for insight and understanding. Some of the great devotional writings of church history provide a tremendous source of spiritual nourishment (think of Bunyan's *The Pilgrim's Progress*, Thomas à Kempis' *The*

Imitation of Christ, The Spiritual Exercises of Ignatius of Loyola and so on). We can also follow the exhortation of the apostle Paul and choose those things that are uplifting as we find them in art, music and literature: 'Finally, brothers, whatever is true, whatever is noble, whatever is right, whatever is pure, whatever is lovely, whatever is admirable – if anything is excellent or praiseworthy – think about such things' (Philippians 4:8).

Henri Nouwen has written a moving account of how God spoke to him through Rembrandt's painting, *The Return of the Prodigal Son*. He first saw it as a poster in someone's office and sensed that God was speaking to him through the painting. As he meditated further on it and visited the museum in Russia where the original is on display, it opened up for him a whole new understanding of what it means to be God's beloved child. He saw himself as both the younger son and the older brother, but sensed also the challenge to become the compassionate father. It was a transforming experience for him and, since then, through his writings, for many others as well.[84]

The fruits of meditation can be seen in a renewed mind and a changed life. If we allow the word of God to be continually in our minds, it will shape the way we think and guide the way we behave. If we allow it to sink into our hearts, it will become part and parcel of who we are, so that obedience to God will become the most natural thing of all. Not surprisingly, meditation easily moves into prayer and opens up a conversation with God. Our meditation takes place in his presence and soon becomes a meditation of him and with him. We should not take the experience for granted, however. Sometimes we will move easily into the presence of God through our meditation; at other times it may not come so easily. We must remember that it is a divine work, for which we are dependent upon God. Thomas Merton warns us, 'Anyone who imagines he can simply begin meditating without praying for the desire and the grace to do so will soon give up. But the desire to meditate, and the grace to begin meditating, should be taken as an implicit promise of further graces.'[85]

Meditation will draw us closer to God and bring God closer to us. It is well worth the effort, and persistence will bring rich rewards.

Lectio divina

Closely linked to the practice of meditation is an ancient method of Bible reading known as *lectio divina* (pronounced lex-ee-oh di-vee-nuh). It has been followed in the church for nearly 1500 years, being first promoted and encouraged by St Benedict among those who followed his Rule. It is a method that is currently returning to popularity.

Essentially, *lectio divina* is a devotional way of reading the scriptures, aiming unashamedly to generate spiritual nourishment rather than academic or intellectual information. It is a way of listening to God with the heart rather than the head. The name means literally 'divine reading' – 'divine' because the subject matter is God's word, and 'reading' since the method involves reading a short passage or verse of scripture several times. It combines both approaches to meditation that we looked at earlier: murmuring to oneself, and silent inward pondering. The purpose is to hear the voice of God through what is read. Norvene Vest explains:

> Lectio is undertaken in the conviction that God's word is meant to be a 'good' word – that is, something carrying God's own life in a way that is beneficial to the one who receives it faithfully. Lectio turns to the Scripture in order that we may be nourished, comforted, refreshed by it. Lectio is an encounter with the living God. It is prayer.[86]

The method behind *lectio divina* is quite simple but very profound. Rather than trying to make sense of the word of God, we simply rest and allow it to speak to us. The word we receive then becomes a 'given' word, purely for our own benefit and for the nourishment of our own souls.

Richard Peace, in his book *Contemplative Bible Reading*, describes a four-part movement in lectio divina, which I quote in full below.

1 **Reading/listening**: Read aloud a short passage of scripture. As you read, listen for the word or phrase that speaks to you. What is the Spirit drawing your attention to?
2 **Meditating**: Repeat aloud the word or phrase to which you are drawn. Make connections between it and your life. What is God saying to you by means of this word or phrase?
3 **Praying**: Now take these thoughts and offer them back to God in prayer, giving thanks, asking for guidance, asking for forgiveness, and resting in God's love. What is God leading you to pray?
4 **Contemplating**: Move from the activity of prayer to the stillness of contemplation. Simply rest in God's presence. Stay open to God. Listen to God. Remain in peace and silence before God. How is God revealing himself to you?[87]

Peace is quick to point out that *lectio divina* is not a substitute for serious Bible study or for understanding the text in an academic way. Rather, it builds upon the analytical approach and, to some extent, assumes a reasonably good knowledge of scripture. It has a different objective in mind, however – helping us to hear God's word through the text and to grow in holiness of life as a result. Certainly it provides a welcome alternative for those who study the Bible professionally in order to prepare sermons, Bible studies, talks and so on. It gives a framework for approaching God in the simplicity of faith and allowing him to speak directly to us rather than through the efforts of intellectual study.

Lectio divina can also be used in a group setting, although the contemplative aspect is normally omitted, since, by nature, that is a more personal experience. For group use, Norvene Vest, in *Knowing By Heart*, provides an excellent summary:

The basic process for our group lectio is roughly this:

(1) The leader reads a short passage from Scripture, and in silence the group members listen attentively for a particular word or phrase that seems to be given to each. Then each simply speaks aloud the word received.

(2) Another member reads the same passage a second time, and in silence the group members ponder how the passage seems to touch their lives. Then each person briefly speaks aloud his or her sense of being touched.

(3) The same passage is read a third time, and in silence group members reflect on a possible invitation found in the passage to do or be something in the next few days. Each person speaks of the invitation he or she has received.

(4) Finally the group members each pray in turn that the person to his or her right be empowered to do or to be what he or she feels called to do or to be.[88]

Both Peace and Vest provide further helpful instructions about how to follow *lectio divina* effectively, individually and in the context of a group. Peace suggests that, in a postmodern context, *lectio divina* will grow in popularity as it offers an experiential alternative to a purely cognitive approach to Bible study. Certainly, whenever I introduce this approach to listening to God through the scriptures, it is enthusiastically received.

One Sunday evening, I was preaching in a local church. As the time drew near for me to speak, I grew more and more certain that I should not give the address I had prepared but, rather, lead the congregation in a corporate lectio divina exercise. Knowing that this particular group was not afraid to try new things, I decided to follow what I felt was a prompting of the Holy Spirit.

I explained that, rather than serving up yet another precooked meal for them from God's word, I wanted to teach them how to hear God for themselves simply by listening to the reading of scripture. That seemed to win their attention, for they realised that they could not just sit back and listen to what I had to say about the passage: they would have to engage with it for themselves.

I chose a short passage from Psalm 27 and slowly read it aloud three times. When the opportunity came to share which words or phrases had had most impact on them, several people immediately shared with the rest of the congregation. It was obvious that they were hearing from God, very clearly, very personally and also very easily. The church minister himself said that God had spoken to him through the words 'all the days of my life' (v. 4). Afterwards he shared more fully with me.

Apparently he had just celebrated his 40th birthday, a milestone for anyone, and was conscious of wanting to make the most of his life in service to God. Those simple words had touched him at his point of need and had become a means by which he was enabled to offer himself and his service again to God for the rest of his life. It was a simple but profound interaction with the word of God, made possible by the reading of scripture.

On most occasions when I have taken part in *lectio divina* myself, I have found that God has invariably spoken to me clearly and I have had no difficulty in remembering what he has said. Somehow the word goes straight to my heart. When I compare this experience to the number of sermons I have heard and soon forgotten, it makes me think I should be using *lectio divina* more often.

14

Contemplation

I first met the girl who would become my wife when we were students at Bible college. We were assigned to the same church at the weekends and soon realised we had a lot in common. As our relationship developed, we would meet for a supper drink in the college dining-room after the evening study period was over.

College was very strict in those days and the women's accommodation block was out of bounds, so, to let Evelyn know that I had finished my studies, I would creep round to the back of the building and tap on her window. Fortunately she was on the ground floor. Sometimes, though, before letting her know I was there, I would simply stand and gaze admiringly for a minute or two as she sat at her desk studying. That's how you know you are in love – when even a simple glimpse of the other makes your heart leap!

Contemplation has been described in somewhat similar terms as 'the prayer of loving attentiveness' or 'the prayer of loving regard'. It has been defined as the gaze of the soul upon God. In its essence, it is about loving God and allowing ourselves to be loved by him.

To contemplate means 'to look steadily at'. When we contemplate something, we give it our full attention – whether it is a beautiful panorama, an arresting piece of music, a work of art or an aspect of nature. In Christian contemplation we are looking at Jesus and beholding or considering him. In silence and stillness we give attention to the one who is the Lover of our souls. The focus moves away from self and fixes itself adoringly upon him.

In biblical terms, contemplation is the experience of entering into the Most Holy Place, drawing near to God and knowing him drawing near to us. This, according to the letter to the Hebrews, is the reason Christ died – to bring us to God. No longer is God distant and remote. The curtain that separated us has been torn in two. We can come near with boldness and confidence (see Hebrews 10:19–22).

Exactly where meditation ends and contemplation begins is not always clear. Many people use the terms interchangeably anyway, and, in some ways, they are almost inseparable. Yet there is an important difference between them. While meditation is like the journey, contemplation is like the arrival point. In meditating, we are seeking to make ourselves aware of God and to warm our hearts towards him; in contemplation, having already become aware of his presence, we are enjoying him, delighting ourselves in all that he is to us. Meditation helps us reach the point at which contemplation begins. Joyce Huggett says, 'Contemplation goes further and deeper than meditation. While the person meditating mutters and muses on God's word, the contemplative pays silent attention to Jesus, the living Word – the one who is central to their prayer.'[89]

It is easy to get the impression from some spiritual writings that contemplation is the 'high point' in Christian experience, attainable by only a very few fortunate individuals of the highest spiritual calibre. There is sometimes too sharp a distinction made between 'the active way' and the 'contemplative way'. Often the mystical aspects are overemphasised, and analogies of 'ascent' and an 'upward' journey suggest that contemplation is reserved for a spiritual elite.

Alexander Ryrie, in his excellent book *Silent Waiting*, is quick to dismiss such an approach and to stress that contemplation is the provenance of all. 'Contemplative prayer… refers to the practice of praying silently rather than in words, of entering an inner silence and stillness in order to be open to God. This is a way of prayer which is available to all, regardless of how far up the spiritual mountain they may have climbed.'[90]

Contemplation cannot be distinguished from prayer. Contemplation is prayer, albeit a particular form of prayer. In contemplative prayer we do not need to ask for anything. Petitionary prayer has its place, as does intercession, but contemplative prayer goes beyond asking God for things to the place where we simply rest in God. Ryrie says, 'In it we ask for nothing – not even for any experience of God, for any progress in the spiritual life, for any growth in goodness, or for any benefit for ourselves or others – but we simply concentrate on God alone.'[91]

God's presence is often associated with silence, and it follows that a deepening relationship with him will bring us into the realm of silence. God does use words to communicate but he is not bound by them. Indeed, human words remain inadequate for the deepest levels of communication, and often get in the way of what we are trying to say. The profoundest revelation often takes place not through conscious thought or mental agility but simply by 'being with' God. Ryrie again has a helpful comment: 'His will or his word can become effective in us not only through the ideas of our heads but more profoundly through our being in his presence. God communicates most deeply through communion.'[92]

Perhaps this is one of the sticking points for those who are used to a more cerebral approach to understanding God. Contemplative spirituality is a spirituality of the 'heart', by which is meant not the seat of the emotions but a person's spiritual centre, their innermost being – in Paul's word, their 'spirit' (1 Thessalonians 5:23; 1 Corinthians 14:14–16; Romans 8:16). God is to be apprehended not with mental faculties but with spiritual ones, with what Paul described as 'the eyes of your heart' (Ephesians 1:18). Contemplative writers often use such expressions as 'descending into the heart' or 'putting the mind into the heart'. What they mean is that, in contemplating God, the natural mind has its limitations. We cannot know God through intelligence; we can only know about God (see 1 Corinthians 1:21). Direct, first-hand, life-changing knowledge of God comes only through revelation, and that comes to the centre of a person – the 'heart'.

It is important to remember at this point that contemplation is not something we do ourselves, unaided. We need the help of God. It is not a psychological technique that we learn, and we cannot make it happen; it is a movement of grace in our hearts and comes to us as pure gift.

Thomas Merton, one of the most respected contemplative writers, regarded contemplation as the work of the Holy Spirit within us, a gift given to all God's children if they wished to receive it, and given with the purpose of intensifying our awareness of God's love for us. He was convinced that the majority of Christians have no idea of the immensity of the love of God for them, or of the power of that love to do them good, to bring them happiness.

Contemplatives often speak of 'infused' prayer – that is, prayer which is poured into us by God and received as a gift. St Teresa of Avila, for example, stressed that contemplative prayer was divinely produced, a wordless awareness and love that can be neither initiated nor prolonged. It comes simply as a gift of grace. It is the love of God being shed abroad in our hearts by the Holy Spirit (Romans 5:5).

It is interesting to note the similarity between some descriptions of contemplative prayer ('an in-loveness felt and experienced') and the way in which some charismatics describe their experience of being filled with the Spirit as 'falling in love with Jesus'. Certainly, when I look back to the time when I had such an experience, it was a sense of being overwhelmed by the love of God. I knelt in prayer by my bedside, hungry to know God more deeply and conscious of standing at the edge of a vast ocean, yet afraid to let myself go. Eventually I was able to do so, and at once I was enveloped in a wave of divine love and acceptance. It was God's doing, though, not mine.

Likewise, it seems to me that what many Christians call 'soaking prayer' is in fact a contemporary expression of contemplation – an opportunity to rest in God's love and relax in his presence. Without knowing the terminology, they are almost certainly experiencing the 'infused' prayer of which contemplatives speak. Perhaps there is a much closer overlap between charismatic experience and contemplative prayer than we may have realised; perhaps here is a meeting point between the two traditions.

The awareness that contemplation is a gift, rather than an art we have to learn, is extremely liberating. It makes what we are seeking attainable, since the initiative lies with God. It is not so much a matter of our finding God but of our being found by him. It is not God who is elusive, but us. As Bishop Stephen Verney writes:

> This is the nature of the encounter, not that I am stumbling towards Abba Father, but that the Abba Father is running towards me. It is not that I love God, but that God loves me; not that I believe in God, but that he believes in me. The discovery at the heart of contemplation is not that I am contemplating the divine love, but that divine love is contemplating me. God sees me and understands me, accepts me, has compassion on me, creates me afresh from moment to moment, and he protects me.[93]

These are profound words, which will repay careful meditation, for they open up before us the possibility of a new and deeper awareness of God and his love for us. It is not my love for God that is the mainspring of contemplative prayer, but his prior, unending and unchanging love for me. While I may think of him intermittently, at best, the thoughts he has towards me are without number, whether I wake or sleep (see Psalm 139:17–18).

Of course, this means that there is a certain 'elusiveness' about contemplative prayer. Warm feelings are not always experienced, nor should they always be sought or used as an indicator to gauge the validity of contemplative prayer. There is bound to be a natural ebb and flow in our apprehension of God, and there will inevitably be highs and lows. This is one reason why many contemplatives stress the need for discernment and seek the help of a spiritual director or mentor – so that they are not discouraged when they have dry seasons, and do not feel abandoned when the warm glow disappears.

With this in mind, then, it is easier for us to understand what true contemplation is: the response of our hearts to the call of God to rest in his presence and delight ourselves in his love. We draw near to him by relaxing ourselves and becoming quiet within. We hold ourselves in his presence, aware of the magnitude of his love towards us, leaning ourselves upon him and gazing upon his loveliness. There we remain, silent and content, not saying anything, happy to let him speak if he so desires.

Practical steps

By far the best practical guide I have found to contemplative prayer is *Coming to God in the Stillness* by Jim Borst.[94] He suggests twelve steps that we can follow as a method for contemplative prayer. For simplicity's sake, I have reduced these steps to three phases, but have summarised the content of each step within the phases. It is assumed that anyone wishing to enter into contemplation will be unhurried as far as time is concerned. The feeling of being able to take as much time as is necessary is more important than the actual amount of time available. The essential ingredient is to be focused and unhurried.

The first stage: relaxing

The first challenge is to quieten our hearts, following the call of God to be still and know that he is God (Psalm 46:10). We can do this by slowing ourselves down, breathing slowly and deeply and relaxing our whole bodies. Next, with the encouragement of scripture (1 Peter 5:7), we can hand over our tensions and worries to God, becoming aware that he is present with us. Consciously and deliberately, we give to God the clutter of worries, anxieties and pressures that might keep us from prayer. Writing down how we are feeling may help to release us, and quiet, reflective music may help us unwind. It is important that we are authentic as we come to God. We can begin to call on the name of Jesus or repeat the name 'Abba, Father'. Gradually our hearts will begin to open to God and we will begin to receive his love. It is important not to rush this stage, and on some occasion we may need to spend the whole time at stage one, as we relax ourselves and allow the rest of God to enter us afresh.

The middle stage: drawing closer

Once we know that our heart is awakened to God, we can draw closer, beginning to deal with things that may hinder us from enjoying full communion with God. It may be appropriate to surrender ourselves to God afresh, asking that he would possess us anew. We also need to forgive from the heart. God's mercy and grace flow freely towards us, and we should likewise forgive others. We let go of bitterness, resentment, hurt feelings and anything else that God shows us is a barrier to our intimacy with him. We can repent of our own sin and failure, confessing to God in the knowledge that he forgives and accepts us, without falling into either guilt or a sense of inferiority. At this point, it is good to ask in faith that God would touch us again by his Spirit, seeking a fresh outpouring of his love. On different occasions, the Lord will emphasise different aspects of the process to us during this stage. Again, the important thing is not to rush through them.

The final stage: enjoyment

As the barriers come down, we find our hearts opening up to God more fully and we begin to experience the joy of contemplation, when we are held enraptured by him. His presence is more and more real; he has our attention. This phase may move in any of several directions. It may become a time of receiving from God. It may move into praise and thanksgiving. We may be led to intercede, feeling God's heart for other people and the world. We may simply stay resting in the presence of our Beloved One, basking in the warmth of his love and approval.

It has often been said that the best way to learn how to pray is to pray, and certainly the best way to learn how to contemplate is to contemplate. As we regularly open ourselves up to God in this way, it is bound to have a transforming effect on our lives. We cannot enjoy intimacy with God like this and remain unchanged. Christ's friendship is a transforming friendship.

We can expect to be more relaxed, more at peace and more like Christ. We will be more aware of sin and have a greater hatred for it. We will have a greater realisation that we are loved by God and, as a result, have a greater love for other people. With time, we can expect to become more truly ourselves and find a greater freedom from the hang-ups that may have troubled us in the past. There should be a greater balance in our lives (between rest and work) and we will enjoy our own company more. We may also feel more invigorated for service, but less inclined to run around doing everything as we once did. Most importantly of all, we will be more pleasing to God.

Contemplation sets before us an exciting adventure, the possibility of exploring new dimensions in the love of God. This is what our souls were made for, what they cry out for and long for – to know God more deeply. This was the longing of King David, to see the beauty of the Lord (Psalm 27:4). This was the heart cry of the apostle Paul, 'to know Christ' (Philippians 3:10). It is the true yearning of all in whom the Spirit of God dwells, 'who have set their hearts on pilgrimage' (Psalm 84:5).

Living freely and lightly

Where do we go from here? If the Spirit really is calling us to an integration of contemplative spirituality within the activism of the evangelical and charismatic streams, what are the implications? The most significant seems to be that we must be able to work out our spirituality within the demands of life today. Can busy people really be contemplative? Can we learn to live freely and lightly in this day and age?

15

Spirituality for busy people

During my time working at Bawtry Hall, a missions training centre in the north of England, I was granted a three-month sabbatical from my work. I was looking forward to a time of concentrated study and some much-needed peace and quiet. The first day of my leave coincided with the commencement of renovation work in the bathroom of our home. We expected it to last two weeks, and I felt I would be able to put up with the noise and some minor inconveniences for such a short time. Little did I realise all that could go wrong on such a project.

Three months later, as my sabbatical came to an end, the bathroom was finished at last. There had been many disappointments, many frustrations and many hassles along the way. We'd had to contend with inadequate workmen, unexpected delays, leaking pipes and broken fittings. We were without central heating for ten days during a cold spell. The bathroom was unusable for days on end. If ever I thought my time aside would transport me to another dimension of heavenly living, I was wrong. But then, that's what real life is all about, isn't it? We must be able to work out our faith in the context of a real and often trying world.

Whatever form our spirituality takes, it has to be related to everyday life. A rediscovery of contemplative spirituality offers the possibility of restoring balance and harmony to lives that are overcrowded and far too hectic. It must also, however, be integrated into the whole of life as it is lived in the day-to-day.

Some people feel that contemplative spirituality holds the danger of becoming a 'spirituality of withdrawal'. While recognising the value of times of solitude and aloneness for the nurture of the spirit, they argue, quite rightly, that there must be a connection with the things that normally occupy and preoccupy the majority of us. They call for a 'domestic spirituality', by which they mean a spirituality that can be expressed in the home and family, the workplace and office. Simon Holt comments, 'Spirituality is about all of life and all of who we are. It has to do with moments of retreat and rush-hour traffic, with periods of silence and the noise of little children, with the communion table and the work bench, with hushed Sunday worship and frantic family dinners.'[95]

Eugene Peterson's paraphrase of John 1:14 lends weight to this point of view, illustrating graphically for us the reality of Christ's incarnation and the depth of his identification with us: 'The Word became flesh and blood, and moved into the neighbourhood.'

Although Jesus certainly practised times of 'strategic withdrawal' throughout his ministry, he never cut himself off from people or their needs. He lived his life before them in the cut-and-thrust of human existence, and he calls us to do the same. He could be seen, heard and touched. His teaching drew on imagery straight from the everyday lives of his hearers. It was no abstract philosophical message that he preached, but one soaked in the real concerns of ordinary people. The incarnation reminds us of the possibility of spiritual living in the domestic settings of our earthly lives.

It may be true, also, that contemplative spirituality can appear out of the reach of ordinary Christians who have little free time and need to concentrate on mundane things such as babies and nappies, earning their living and simply keeping the household going. When you have a busy job and a family to care for, as well as a mortgage to pay off, it is easy to feel less spiritual than those 'full-time' Christians who can give greater attention to seeking God.

Of course, this should not be so. In whatever context we live, we should be able to work out the terms of our discipleship in ways that are realistic and attainable. The parent with young children, the student with exams to pass, the boss with his deadlines, the salesman on the road – each should be able to find a spirituality that works in their situation and draws them closer to God. This is not to say that it will be easy to do so. Perhaps the greatest hindrance is the fact that often we fail and are easily drawn back into our old ways.

It is my conviction, however, that contemplative spirituality can – indeed, must – be integrated into ordinary living. The pace of life is not going to get slower, and many people will need to experience God while travelling 'in the fast lane'. But even there, God is to be found. Amid the pressure and the turmoil, the stress and the strain, we can encounter him as genuinely as in the most sacred cathedral.

How can this happen? It will be helpful first to consider the level of our desire for God. To find God, we must want God. If our desire for God is currently low, it may be because something or someone has taken the place of God in our lives. Adjustment may be necessary. Otherwise, we may need to ask God to increase the desire within us. In my experience, hunger for God makes room for itself. If we truly long for God, we will make time for him, no matter how crowded our lives may be.

Then we must be willing to undertake a thoroughgoing re-evaluation of the way we live. I hope that all we have explored in this book will have helped us to recognise the value and importance of silence and solitude, and their significance for our well-being, both physical and spiritual. Without a radical shift in our values, we will not have the willingness to change established behaviour patterns. However, if we are convinced that it is essential to find time and space for God and to build periods of reflection into our lives, even in our busy schedules we may find room.

It will also be good to review how we are using our time and to ask ourselves some searching questions. Why am I so busy? What drives me to attend so many meetings, to be involved in so many activities? Is my workaholic tendency covering up some underlying issue that I am afraid to face? What am I trying to prove? Above all, we need to ask the question, 'Is there anything that I could prune from my diary?' If we are willing to be radical, we may well find that we have more time and space available to us than we realised, and our lives may become less cluttered and more easily managed.

It may also be timely to consider our image of God, and the basis on which we relate to him. How do we think of God? Do we see him as an ever-demanding employer, paying low wages and demanding long hours? Or is he a despotic Pharaoh, asking us to make bricks without straw and treating us like slaves? Is he a God who is never satisfied, never pleased with us, never smiling? Even mature Christians often live with distorted ideas of God.

In order to make time for God, we have to want to be with him. If we understand what he is truly like, we shall long for his presence. Remember, God is full of intense love towards us and only wants to do good in our lives. He welcomes us unconditionally and desires the very best for us. He is full of mercy and grace, and would do nothing to hurt or harm us. He is our Shepherd, Saviour and Friend, and longs to be with us.

We are to relate to God on the basis of his grace towards us. I can come to him just as I am and know that I will be welcomed and accepted. Even if I have failed and have not lived up to my own best standards, I can still draw near. I don't have to earn my acceptance or achieve the right to be there. I can come boldly and confidently because God himself has provided a way by which I can draw near to him. I come not on the basis of my own goodness (I have none anyway), but on the basis of my position in Christ.

Strategies for finding God

Having undertaken a review like this, we can now build into our lives certain strategies that will help us experience God more frequently in the midst of the maelstrom of life.

Firstly, we can find God as we learn to 'practise the presence of God'. We associate this expression with Brother Lawrence. He was a 17th-century monk in France who found himself, somewhat reluctantly, assigned to kitchen duties on a regular basis. Rather than complaining, however, he gave himself wholeheartedly to the task of serving God where he was, and right there, among the pots and pans, he learned to 'practise the presence of God'. So remarkable was his serenity in the midst of the steamy kitchens that he became something of a celebrity, with both rich and famous coming to meet him and learn the secret of his peacefulness. It was, of course, the fact that he was constantly aware of God's presence with him, even as he did the washing up, that brought such calmness to his spirit. 'God is everywhere,' he is recorded as saying, 'in all places, and there is no spot where we cannot draw near to him, and hear him speaking in our heart: with a little love, just a very little, we shall not find it hard.'[96]

What Brother Lawrence discovered in the kitchens, we can find on the shopfloor or in the nursery, the office or the classroom. God is with us wherever we are and whatever we are doing, and at any moment we can enter into dialogue with him. Busy days can be filled with his presence. Even earthly stables can become his dwelling place.

We live in a God-bathed world. There is no place where God is not, although sometimes we may be asleep to his presence. This is why we need what writer Timothy Jones calls 'awakenings'.[97] These are divinely given moments in our days when we become aware of the activity and nearness of God. Suddenly, in the midst of another humdrum day, we see the traces of divine presence. It may be in words that are spoken, an incident that takes place, a thought that comes to us or something that makes us laugh or cry – and suddenly we are aware of God. He is in the moment, and an ordinary event has become an epiphany. The more 'awake' we become, the more we recognise that our days contain many such moments; all we need are eyes to see them. God has impregnated our world with himself. What we need is to be attentive to him.

Secondly, we can find God in the world around us. The Celtic Christians were particularly 'alive' to the presence of God. For them, life was lived in the atmosphere of God's nearness. Whether milking the cow or copying the scriptures, all was divine activity; all was sacred. Everything took place within the overshadowing presence of God. The Lord was there all around them in the beauty of nature – in the seas and skies, in the fish and the birds, in the mountains and coastlines. For them, there was no distinction between sacred and secular. God was all and in all.

We need to rediscover this 'holistic' approach to life, for God is more present in our own sophisticated world than we imagine. The world around us offers plenty of opportunity to encounter God. As the children's hymn says, 'Around me when I look, his handiwork I see; this world is like a picture book, to tell his love to me.'[98] How often do we stop to read it? It is there all around us, declaring the glory of God. The challenge is to walk through life with our eyes wide open to the presence and activity of God, expecting to encounter him in our daily living.

Such a possibility is open to us all. Even as we travel around in the midst of our busyness, we can see the handiwork of God. In the city centre it is there: in the trees, the birds, the people, the colours, the sky, the rain, the bricks, the shape of the buildings and much more. 'Wherever I live,' says Timothy Jones, 'whatever the time of year, what I see, taste, and touch can point my soul, if I let it, to a new awareness of God's creative goodness.'[99]

Thirdly, we can find God as we sanctify our work. Whatever work we are given to do (whether paid or voluntary, at home or in a place of work), we can see it as our calling and do it for the glory of God. Such an attitude transforms our work and brings God right into the centre of our lives. After all, most of our time is taken up with work in one form or another, and it is unthinkable to leave God out of such a major part of our lives. If I know I am doing it for him, it is as much 'service' as any 'spiritual' form of activity. My work is dignified and I can feel his pleasure in what I do. However menial the task, however mundane the job, if I seek to glorify God in it, then it can be considered as important to God.

We can also expect to see God at work within our work. He will use the circumstances of our work to shape and mould our character, for he is just as much sovereign over what happens there as anywhere else. No moment of our day and no part of our life is outside his control. Of course, we can also bring God into our working environment by thinking of him and praying quietly, as we get the opportunity. He is interested in the details of our work, since anything that is a concern to us is a concern to him. In this way, we can operate on two levels at once, living concurrently, by keeping one eye on heaven while we are firmly engaged on earth.

It may not be easy to maintain such a spiritual orientation, but it is possible. We can soak our work with our prayer. Our work can be our worship as we offer what we do to God and as we seek to remain aware of him throughout the day.

Fourthly, we can find God as we learn to pace ourselves. Enjoying the presence of God has to do with leaving spaces in our lives, with not overcrowding ourselves. This is partly to do with good planning and partly to do with creating an appropriate rhythm in our lives. It is important to find patterns that fit us, rather than establishing rigid systems for ourselves. After all, we are seeking to nurture a relationship with a person, not run a programme. We need to understand how we function best – what works for us and what doesn't. Then we can seek to alternate between work and rest, activity and prayer, time with God and time with others.

It is rather like a large wheel with a hub at the centre. Part of us (the rim) is in touch with the ground – that is, the ordinary demands of daily life. This is the part that is moving. The hub, however, is at the centre and remains still. This is our heart, or spirit, which is in tune with God. Thus we combine both busyness and stillness. Our activities revolve around a still axis, and this is what creates balance and harmony in our lives.

In this context, I have found particularly helpful the insights of David Kundtz in his book *Stopping*.[100] He describes three ways of being still even when we have to keep going. He calls them still points, stopovers and grinding halts.

Even the busiest of lives has its quiet moments, its 'still points'. We have to recognise them and make use of them. Coffee breaks, lunch hours, travelling time or walks between offices can all provide us with little moments of solitude that can nourish our souls. Sometimes we have to choose to leave the crowd and be alone. These little pools of silence are kingdom moments, given by God so that we can turn our hearts towards him. They take us from the rim to the hub.

Many people find it helpful to frame their day more deliberately with a short period (say, 15 minutes) for quiet meditation and prayer. This regular pattern helps to establish within them a 'still centre' out of which they can operate for the rest of the day. It gives a focus to their lives and helps them to set priorities. From this place of rest they can respond more efficiently to whatever chaos lies around them.

Sometimes a group of friends with a shared desire for God can arrange to meet together. At one period in my life, I had the opportunity to attend such a group that met weekly during the lunch hour. After a short time of devotion, often using a simple liturgy, we did *lectio divina* together and finished with a few minutes of quiet prayer. I doubt if I would have managed it on my own, but, with the encouragement of others and the framework provided by those who hosted the meeting, I was able to find an opportunity for stillness in the midst of my busy timetable. Meeting with others is also a valuable antidote to becoming too individualistic in our relationship with God.

As well as daily times of stillness, we need to be renewed through more leisurely periods of quiet. These are the 'stopovers' and can be achieved with careful forethought and determination. We need to commit ourselves to them, not leaving them as a vague good intention for 'when the time is right': it will never be right. A day away on our own can provide much-needed space. Parents with small children can make a 'gift' of such a day to each other occasionally. Such opportunities are like an oasis when you have a young family.

Longer periods – the 'grinding halts' – may be taken for retreat as well, realising that such time away is not a luxury but a necessity. Here we are thinking of two or three days at a time, even longer for those who have the appetite and desire. These breaks are not the extravagances of a selfish life but the essentials for a balanced one. Holidays were originally meant to be 'holy days', and, if we bear this is mind, it may well be possible for some of us to use our time off work to enrich our walk with God. It is worth reflecting, too, that God in his love has a way of making us take enforced rest from time to time. If we won't commit ourselves to do it, he may well, in his mercy, impose it on us through sickness or other circumstances.

The principle of sabbath still holds good, and we neglect it at our spiritual and emotional peril: many of those who have suffered burn-out thought they were exempt. If God was concerned for the ground to lie fallow (Exodus 23:11), how much more is he concerned that we, his children, have proper rest and recreation and the chance to be still? So we incorporate into our hectic schedules pauses when we can spend time at the 'hub', receiving a fresh inflow of divine life. We learn to pace ourselves.

A friend decided to take a day for prayer and fasting, hoping to combine it with his work responsibilities. He managed the fasting but, unfortunately, that particular day was fraught with unexpected difficulties and demands, and he failed to pray. He was disappointed, feeling that he had let himself and God down. Such an experience illustrates the difficulty of finding a spirituality that works for busy people.

My friend did not appreciate, though, that he was thinking of prayer in a limited way – either as vocal prayer or as prayer formed in the mind. He perhaps failed to realise that God reads our hearts and knows our desires, whether or not we manage to express them outwardly. Prayer is not just an activity that we do; it is a relationship that we live, an attitude of our hearts. Because he was living within the presence of God, his prayer was heard, because he is his prayer. God knows the desires of our heart.

Because of the nature of my work, I spend a lot of time travelling, often driving up and down the motorways. I find that I really enjoy these times, cocooned away from phone calls and emails, freed to enjoy my own company and think my own thoughts. Such journeys provide me with a natural opportunity for solitude and give me an oasis of calm in my busyness. Sometimes I listen to the radio (traffic reports are essential!), often I will put on some worship music and enjoy singing praise to God, and occasionally I will simply benefit from some prayerful thinking time. Such times happen naturally and have become special for me. It is one of the rhythms of grace that the Spirit has helped me to build into my own life, and it helps to keep me centred on Jesus and abiding in him. It's nothing profound or revolutionary, just a simple habit that has evolved in the midst of a busy life lived on the move.

This is what contemplative spirituality is all about, and it works, even in the busiest of lives. I don't always live up to my own ideals but, when I fail, I try not to be discouraged and try to see it all as a learning process. The important thing is to make the effort. If we want to find time to be with God, we can do so. We will need to be creative, disciplined and determined, but it is possible.

16

The dream

I had been speaking at a conference on the south coast of England, and, after one of the sessions, was talking informally with a delegate who shared with me something of her own story, and how God had been helping her to live in the rhythms of grace. She felt that God had spoken to her quite profoundly through a dream, and, as a result, she had made significant changes to her whole way of life, especially her pattern of work. I was so moved by what she told me that I asked her permission to share her story with others. Here, in her own words, Beverley Shepherd explains what happened, how she responded and the challenge it presents to us all.

We all dream – or so I'm told – it's just that I don't normally remember mine. So when one morning I awoke with every detail of a dream vividly etched on my memory, I knew that God had spoken.

The dream concerned a rail journey. I was travelling by train to a large city, arriving at one terminus and then needing to continue my journey from a second terminus some way across the city. Bicycles were provided to cross the city, but I had only three minutes to make my connection. I pedalled furiously while clutching a parcel containing something very precious. Worn out, I arrived at the second terminus with time to spare, but had lost the parcel. Still, with my 30 remaining seconds I could retrace my journey and find it – or so I thought. The precious parcel had disappeared, and in its place I collected several other parcels – all jiffy bags full of bubblewrap.

I dashed back to the second terminus and leapt on to the train as it was pulling out of the station. Making my way to a corner seat, I collapsed exhausted, surrounded by my parcels full of nothing. It was then that I awoke.

I knew that the dream had been a warning. 'What was in that first parcel that was so precious?' was my anxious question as I prayed. God showed me something specific. I picked up my diary and started to rearrange my schedule. My diary is not that easy to reorganise, with many events being booked several months in advance. However, six months later, the changes started to bear fruit and I realised with both shock and gratitude that God's warning had come just in time.

The changes I made to my diary reflected the principles of 'working from rest' – of building into my life weekly, monthly and yearly patterns and starting each of these cycles with times of drawing aside to listen to God. That listening involves discerning his priorities and perspective on the work and relationships to which I am called, but first and foremost it is the time when I remember who I am – his beloved daughter in whom he is well pleased. Everything flows from that understanding.

What might you lose if you continue to live at your present pace? Your laughter and spontaneity? Your sense of fun? Your peace? Your vision? Your most cherished relationships? Your intimacy with God? Only you know, and only you can choose to change.

As God speaks, perhaps through the pages of this book, and calls you back to intimacy with himself, it is up to you to respond and take up his gracious invitation. Then, when you come to him, you will discover what true rest is and you too will start to recover your life. You will learn from Jesus the unforced rhythms of grace, and, as you practise them, you will begin to live freely and lightly.

Working it out

The aim of this part of the book is to help you work out in practice the lessons you have been learning as you have read *Rhythms of Grace*. The material is my own and the various 'exercises' have been used in different settings before but never published in this way.

My vision is for these sessions to be worked through by a small group of people (ideally six to twelve) who meet together, either weekly or fortnightly, for the purpose of encouraging each other to incorporate into their daily lives the six spiritual disciplines mentioned in the book, and thereby deepen their walk with God. Not all the material from the book is covered. I have chosen to focus on Chapters 9–14 to make the course achievable for the majority of people. These are the most practically based chapters and the most suitable for application in daily life. It will be helpful, however, if participants read the whole book to understand the bigger picture.

The sessions focus on the six key spiritual disciplines that help us establish a spiritual rhythm in our lives and are fundamental in developing a growing intimacy with God. Stillness, silence and solitude are the disciplines that bring us closer to God, helping us to move from the circumference of life to its centre in him. Reflection, Bible meditation and contemplation are the disciplines that take us further into God, leading us from the shallowness of hurried living into the deeper places of the soul where God is to be encountered more fully.

Each session has three key parts:

- Understanding: here I try to establish a simple biblical rationale for each of the disciplines.
- Practising together: here we look at ways by which we may familiarise ourselves with each discipline in the context of the group meeting.
- Practising by yourself: here I offer suggestions for taking things forward personally, as individuals seek to make each discipline a part of their life.

Additionally, the first three sessions include a section called 'Seeking'. Here my aim is to show the relevance of stillness, silence and solitude to our lives, and to help group members think through why these disciplines will be beneficial for them.

I envisage that each session can be completed in 60–75 minutes. I have deliberately tried not to be too prescriptive about the format of each session, so that individual groups can establish their own pattern to sit easily with the ethos of who they are as people and where they are on their spiritual journey. Feel free to use this material in the way that works best for you.

A home will be an ideal meeting place, but any venue that is comfortable and peaceful will be suitable. Creative people might like to make a display or sacred space that fits with the theme of each session.

I have not included directions for group leaders, as many other books do this and it is easy to find guidance on leading a small group if you need it.

The emphasis of the sessions is on learning together, but it may be helpful to have a time of worship at the beginning or end. Let this be a time for quiet, reflective worship, perhaps with a mixture of free worship and some simple liturgy, like the Northumbria

Prayer (available from northumbriacommunity.org), or the ones on pages 148–150. Three things may be especially helpful as you get underway:

- I would encourage everyone who is taking part to make a commitment to attend each session unless there is good reason not to be there. This gives cohesion and stability to the group and allows sharing together to develop more easily. Seeing a process through to the end also aids the learning experience and is a good character builder.
- I would also encourage each participant to start a journal from the beginning and to use it throughout the course, but in a way that fits with who they are as a person: some are more disciplined than others, and some enjoy writing while others don't. It will be important, therefore, for each person to read the relevant section on journalling in Chapter 12.
- Finally, I would encourage you to adopt a system of spiritual friendship or accompaniment as you follow the course, so that each person has someone with whom they can link up, to talk about their progress and to share confidentially if necessary. This might be done in pairs or triplets.

A warning and an invitation

Do remember that no study course provides us with magic answers. Spiritual growth is a process that takes time and requires personal application and discipline. These sessions will not change you overnight or provide instant solutions, but they will give you a starting-point and a measure of impetus so that you will continue pursuing intimacy with God.

Also, take into account that I have deliberately separated the six disciplines so that they can be examined individually. In reality, though, they overlap and cannot be isolated so neatly. Because of this, there will be some measure of overlap in the studies. When the disciplines are integrated into our lives, we discover that we use them together, not separately, and often they merge into each other without distinction.

One final word: I welcome feedback on this material, and would like to hear of your experiences as you use the material. I would also love to receive any ideas you have for teaching the disciplines to others creatively. We have a God who is full of ideas and I'm sure that, as you use the course, he will give you fresh insights that may be of help to others, myself included.

A simple liturgy for seeking God together

The leader speaks the words in bold type. The prayer-poem can be read by one person or, verse by verse, by different individuals. As you share this liturgy, take your time and savour the words. Don't be afraid to pause and reflect at any point. Some quiet instrumental music may lead into the liturgy and may also be used at the end.

Exhortations:

Be still and know that I am God.
He will be exalted among the nations,
he will be exalted in the earth.

The Lord is in his holy temple.
Let all the earth be silent.

Find rest, O my soul, in God alone.
My hope comes from him.
He alone is my rock and my salvation;
he is my fortress. I shall not be shaken.

I have stilled and quietened myself,
just like a small child with its mother.
Yes, like a small child is my soul within me.

One thing I ask of the Lord,
this is what I seek:
that I may dwell in the house of the Lord
all the days of my life,
to behold the beauty of the Lord,
to seek him in his temple.

Those who wait upon the Lord
shall renew their strength.
They will soar on wings like eagles;
they will run and not grow weary;
they will walk and not faint.

I am still confident of this:
I will see the goodness of the Lord
in the land of the living.
Wait for the Lord.
Be strong and take heart.
Wait for the Lord.

A moment of silent meditation:

Jacob's well was there, and Jesus, tired as he was from the journey, sat down by the well. It was about the sixth hour (John 4:6).

A prayer-poem:

In the stillness of this moment
as we seek again your face,
in the beauty of this quiet
may we know once more your grace.
For your love is without measure
and your mercy knows no bounds.
Come surround us with the Father's strong embrace.

As we gaze upon your beauty
and behold your loveliness,

as we turn our eyes toward you
may we glimpse your holiness.
For your love is without measure
and your mercy knows no bounds.
Come transform us with the Son's sweet fruitfulness.

When we meet a world that's broken
and we feel its pain and woe,
will you send us out in power?
Will you show us where to go?
For your love is without measure
and your mercy knows no bounds.
Come immerse us in the Holy Spirit's flow.

Blessing:

**May the blessing of God the Father
be with you;**
may he guard you, guide you and protect you.

**May the blessing of God the Son
be around you;**
may he save you, deliver you and heal you.

**May the blessing of God the Spirit
be upon you;**
may he equip you, anoint you and empower you.

Say together:

May the blessing of the thrice holy God,
Father, Son and Holy Spirit,
be yours in great abundance. Amen

1 Stillness: the opportunity to slow down

Understanding stillness

Read Psalm 46 together, and share your responses to the following questions:

- What appears to be the context of this psalm? What's going on in the background?
- What is it about God that seems to calm the people down?

With this in mind, read aloud together verse 10. What would these words have meant to those who heard them first? How do they speak to you today?

Being still is about slowing down and learning to relax in order to get to know God more fully. If we are always rushing around we will live on the surface of life. Stillness helps us to find a deeper place within ourselves, and also with God.

Read John 4:6 and consider the picture of Jesus sitting by the well and doing nothing. What does this say to you? What can we learn from his example?

Most of us feel guilty if we are not always on the go, doing something worthwhile and being productive. We hate to feel we are 'wasting' time. Jesus was human, just like us. He needed to rest, and his example gives us permission to slow down, too.

Seeking stillness

Many of us are conscious that our lives are too full and that we never seem to have enough time. We sense that there must be a better way to live, but are not sure how to find it or if it is even possible.

Think back over your week. When did you find yourself rushing? When did you feel pressurised for time? On the other hand, when did you feel most relaxed and at peace?

From the following list, underline the words that best describe how you feel most often, and circle the words that describe you least:

bored	frustrated	overwhelmed	relaxed	calm
panicky	tense	stretched	rushed	agitated
heavy laden	tired	energetic	weary	peaceful
worn out	carefree	overloaded	serene	burdened

Share with the group your chosen words, and anything that strikes you from this exercise.

What are your thoughts and feelings as you approach the discipline of stillness?

Practising stillness together

1 Play a piece of gentle instrumental music and listen to it together in silence. Listen carefully to the music, allowing it to draw you into its atmosphere. Seek to become absorbed in the melody. Try to identify the different instruments. Lose yourself in its beauty.

2 Read aloud 1 Peter 5:7: 'Cast all your anxiety on him because he cares for you.' On a piece of paper, make a list of anything that causes you to be anxious and may prevent you from being able to still yourself in God's presence. Hand over your list to God by taking it and placing it in a symbolic place.

3 Read Psalm 133 and imagine yourself as the little child. Visualise your prayer. What makes you fractious and disturbed? Remind yourself that you are loved, wanted and cared for by God. Allow yourself to be held, to be cradled, to be embraced in the arms of God. Feel yourself relaxing, becoming less tense, until you feel at peace. Stay like this for a few minutes.

4 When the time seems right, share a time of open prayer using sentence prayers – short responses to God that establish a dialogue. Let the prayers come from the heart, expressing your thanksgiving, your faith and trust, your longing and so on. Keep your prayers simple and pray slowly until the wave of prayer subsides. Finish by saying the grace together: 'May the grace of our Lord Jesus Christ and the love of God and the fellowship of the Holy Spirit be with you all, for evermore, Amen.'

5 Share any responses to this time together, remembering that if you have never done this before, it will take a little practice before it seems normal and natural for you.

Practising stillness by yourself during the week

1 Take a day when you do things more slowly – eat more slowly, talk more slowly, walk more slowly, breathe more slowly, read more slowly, drive more slowly. Try not to hurry and, if you do, try to slow down.

2 Practise using the Jesus Prayer, learning to pray according to the rhythm of your breathing (see page 79). You can use it in a variety of settings – as you go to sleep, when you are walking, as you are driving, doing the washing up and so on.

3 Create for yourself a special place where you can relax – perhaps a comfortable armchair in a quiet corner. Use it regularly and practise being still. Gradually it will become a safe haven for you, and a meeting place with God.

4 If you find it really difficult to be still and you feel a strong restlessness inside you, ask God to show you what the root cause may be. Try to get behind the feeling of restlessness, to what causes you to feel that way. Be prepared to share with a close friend and to receive prayer if you wish.

5 Journal any thoughts you have.

2 Silence: the opportunity to listen

Understanding silence

Read Proverbs 10:19 and James 3:9–10. Have you ever regretted anything that you have said? Have you ever been hurt by the words of another? Share examples if possible. Can you see why silence can be helpful?

Read James 1:19 and Proverbs 4:20. Why is it better to listen than to speak? How do you feel when someone truly listens to you? What does this have to say to us about hearing God's voice?

Read Habakkuk 2:20 and Zephaniah 1:7. Why might silence be the most appropriate response to the presence of God?

If possible, watch the *Nooma* DVD by Rob Bell called 'Noise' (Zondervan, 2005). How does this film speak to you? Share your responses.

Seeking silence

We live in a noisy world and are sometimes not even aware of the level of noise around us or the effect it has on us. Noise distracts us, robs us of our peace, prevents us from thinking and can stop us from getting the rest we need. More importantly, it is an irritant to the human spirit, which thrives in stillness and silence. Sometimes we speak of noise 'pollution' because of the negative effect it can have upon us.

What noise do you live with? Look at the list below and identify the sources of noise in your life:

traffic	television	radio	neighbours	children
aircraft	trains	sirens	workmen	shops
animals	alarms	phones	computer games	pubs and clubs

Are there any others that you would add to the list?

Do you ever surround yourself with noise intentionally? Why is this?

Why does silence have negative connotations for some people? Does it have for you?

Would you appreciate more quietness in your life? Which of these words appeals to you the most?

tranquillity	calmness	serenity	peacefulness
placid	unruffled	still	hushed

Practising silence together

1 Begin by stilling yourselves, drawing on your experience from the session on 'Stillness'. Perhaps use some quiet music again, or use the Jesus Prayer (page 79). Alternatively, do a simple relaxation exercise (pages 78–79). Some people find that looking at a lighted candle helps them to concentrate.

2 Let the centring time flow naturally into a time of silence. This doesn't have to be long; sometimes five minutes is enough for beginners. During this time:

- Remind yourself that you are in God's presence, for he is everywhere, and that you are welcomed in his presence because he loves you unconditionally.
- Allow your thoughts to settle down. At first your mind will be restless and all kinds of thoughts might come to you. Don't worry about this: it is normal. Simply push the thoughts to one side, and, if they come back, do the same again.
- Begin to listen for the voice of God. What thoughts come to you that seem to be from God? It may be that you are reminded of a scripture, the words of a song or hymn, or something God has already been saying to you. If so, go with these thoughts and

trust your intuition that it really is God speaking to you and not just your imagination. Jot down what you receive, to muse on later.

- It may be that in the silence a particular noise may stand out for you. Listen to it and ask the Holy Spirit to show you if it has any special significance for you.
- God does not always speak to us directly, and you may receive very little, so be content with that. Let the silence become the companionable silence of friends or lovers. Just enjoy being with God and know that, by being still and quiet before him, you are putting yourself in the place where God can speak to you later, if he wishes.
- Turn whatever thoughts you have had into a prayer as you draw your time of silence to a close.

Practising silence by yourself during the week

1 Have a morning / day / evening when you fast from words. Don't have the TV or radio on; turn off your mobile phone and computer; don't even have background music. Spend a couple of hours in silence. The purpose is not to make anything happen but simply to get used to silence. Perhaps read a little, either the scriptures or the chapter in this book on Silence. Pray as you are able, but don't force yourself. Go for a walk to a quiet place if it helps. Notice how you respond to the silence, and share later with someone you trust.

2 Get up early one morning, about 5am, before the world starts moving again. Once you feel awake, enjoy the stillness and quiet of daybreak. Does it feel different to you? Is it easier to pray? Perhaps use a simple liturgy as a framework for your prayer, or go outside and enjoy the new morning. Go back to bed if you need to, but don't be late for work!

3 Journal any thoughts you have.

3 Solitude: the opportunity to connect

Understanding solitude

Read Mark 1:35 and reflect on the way in which Jesus often withdrew to be alone, using some of the insights from this verse and from Chapter 5 of the book. What can we learn from his example?

Read Mark 6:30–32. What was Jesus trying to teach his disciples at the beginning of their ministry? Why can success in ministry, or the growth of what we are doing, be a danger to us?

Read Song of Songs 2:10–13. The Holy Spirit seems to be calling the church to a closer intimacy with God. Do you hear that voice yourself? In what ways has God been speaking to you? How are you responding? Who or what has to be left behind to answer his call?

Read Mark 9:2. Solitude is not always about being alone. Sometimes a small group of friends can seek solitude together, as in this instance. Why do you think Jesus chose these three disciples in particular to be with him? What connection might there be between their being alone and what happened next? What does this say to us about the significance of solitude?

Seeking solitude

If silence is difficult for many people, solitude is even harder. When we are separated from other people, we find ourselves alone with God, and that can feel uncomfortable. Why is this? Consider the following list of possible reasons. Do any apply to you? Are there others that you would add?

- Shame (feeling bad about who I am)
- Guilt (feeling bad about what I have done)
- Feeling unworthy to be near God
- Feeling afraid of God (what will he ask of me?)

- Unconfessed sin
- Unresolved pain or hurt
- Self-hatred (disliking my own company)
- Thinking that solitude is bad (a punishment)
- Fear of being alone (no friends)
- Equating solitude with loneliness

Personality is also a factor here. Some people are extraverts, energised by being with others and involving themselves in activities and events. Others are introverts, finding their energy by being alone or with close friends, and having time and space to think. Both need solitude. The danger for extraverts is that they may not realise this, and they easily become over-extended and exhausted. The danger for introverts is that they may try to live like extraverts and not acknowledge their greater need for time alone. Which description best fits who you are? What impact do you think this has on your spiritual life?

Practising solitude as a group

'Practising solitude as a group' may seem like a contradiction, but it can work if everyone wants to achieve the same objective.

1 When you meet together, after a time of worship, ask one person to share a short devotional thought from the Bible. Then allow each person to go their own way and think about what has been shared, in silence, for 15–20 minutes. Perhaps the speaker can provide a few simple questions to help the others reflect further on what has been shared. Finally, come together to share your thoughts about the passage and your experience of solitude.
2 Plan to have a quiet day together, either by joining one that has been organised by someone else or by arranging your own. Try to find a suitable venue where it will be easy for you to enjoy a prayerful and peaceful atmosphere (for example, a retreat centre, church building or country hotel).

Practising solitude by yourself during the week

1   Many of those who live alone may already be familiar with solitude and comfortable by themselves; others may still have to befriend the silence and enjoy being alone, recognising some of the benefits it offers. There is a difference between aloneness and loneliness. Think about what that difference might be, and journal your thoughts.

2   Solitude is sometimes an involuntary experience. Think about occasions when you have the opportunity to be alone, and ask that God will help you to see the blessing it can be if you learn to use it positively. Such 'given' times may include:

- travelling alone
- working by oneself
- living or staying alone
- being ill or incapacitated
- being confined to home for some other reason
- unexpected delays and queuing in traffic

Remember that some of Paul's greatest letters came out of his time of imprisonment.

3.   Solitude can also be a voluntary experience. Think about simple ways in which you can find and enjoy some personal space, then deliberately choose to get away from people for some time with God:

- walking the dog
- cutting the grass
- doing household chores
- travelling to work
- coffee breaks and lunch times
- some hobbies
- exercising

- walking in the country
- a quiet day or retreat

Resist the temptation to avoid being by yourself. Embrace and welcome time to reflect, to be quiet and to become more focused on God.

4 Take some time to journal your thoughts.

4 Reflection: the opportunity to notice the activity of God

Reflection is the discipline of taking time to think about what God is doing in our lives, and the ability to recognise his activity in the ordinariness of everyday living.

Understanding reflection

Read Genesis 28:16. Jacob awoke with the realisation that God was closer than he thought. What keeps us from being more aware of the presence of God? What stops you from being more spiritually alert and sensitive?

Read 2 Timothy 2:7. Even when we read the scriptures, we may not always recognise the voice of God. Why is that? What must we do as we read, and what can we expect God to do in response?

Read Ephesians 5:15–16. What do you think Socrates meant when he said, 'The unexamined life is not worth living'? How does that idea connect with what Paul is saying here? Why is it helpful to reflect on our lives – our successes and our failures?

Read Jeremiah 1:11–12. What question did God ask Jeremiah? How did Jeremiah's answer help him to receive the word of the Lord? What do you think he learned from this experience? What does it teach us?

Practising reflection together

1 If circumstances allow, try an awareness walk. Each person goes out for a walk of about 15–20 minutes, praying that God will speak to them as they walk. As you go, use your five senses to encounter the world around you in an intentional way. What do you see and hear? What can you touch, taste and smell? As you become aware of God's world around you, thank him for all he has made, for the glory of his creation and for his power and might.

   Then ask yourself, 'How might God be speaking to me? What could be a parable of nature for me?' Take particular notice of anything that stood out for you, that you were particularly drawn to, or that seemed unusual or surprising. How can it be an object lesson for you?

   As you come back to the group, share what you have discovered. If appropriate, bring back with you something that has spoken to you, to show to the others.

   Pray together that God will give you 'eyes to see' his presence and activity. Ask that this way of looking at the world, and this ability to notice, will become natural and automatic for you.

2 Try a simple form of the Prayer of Examen. This is a way of reviewing our day and asking 'Where was God in my life today?' It is done individually, but you can share afterwards your response to this exercise.

   Think back over the last 24 hours (or a few days, if you wish). Recall what happened, playing back the events of the day as if you were watching a DVD.

   What was most significant? Were there any moments when you felt aware of God's presence or realised he was helping you?

Did God use you in any way? Did you demonstrate the fruit of the Spirit? Were you able to show his compassion and love to anyone?

What was challenging for you during the day? Is there anything you regret saying or doing?

What do you want to give thanks for? What do you want to ask forgiveness for? How do you want to ask God to help you?

3 Celebrate Communion together, using the words of 1 Corinthians 11:23–28 or Luke 24:28–35 as an introduction.

Take a moment to examine yourself. Is there anything you wish to put right with God or with your brothers and sisters in Christ?

As you take the bread, remember that Jesus gave his life for you. Reflect on the enormity of his love for you, which never changes and never diminishes.

As you drink the cup, remember that his blood cleanses you from all sin. Reflect on the grace of total forgiveness that is yours in Christ Jesus.

Practising reflection by yourself during the week

1 This week, ask God to make you more alive and alert to his activity in your life. Expect to see him at work and hear him speaking to you in the ordinariness of your life – in the people you meet, the things that happen, what you see, what you read, where you go and so on.
2 If you have not begun to journal yet, now is a good time to start. Make a note of anything that arises out of your desire to be more aware of God.
3 Find some photos of yourself from childhood to the present day. Spread them out before you and consider the course of your life. Estimate your age in each picture and try to recall what was

happening for you at that stage in life. Consider how you have changed physically over the years. What have been the most enjoyable moments of your life? What have been the saddest? What have been the most character forming? Thank God that he has been with you every step of the way. Commit yourself to him for what lies ahead.

4   If, over the next few days, you have a moment when you become aware that something significant is happening, pause and try to follow Ken Gire's process, as described on page 106: read the moment, reflect on it and then respond to it.

5   Take time to journal.

5   Bible meditation: the opportunity to absorb God's word

Christian meditation is generally based on scripture and is the way in which we allow God's truth to travel from our heads to our hearts, thereby moving our wills to action. It is the discipline of thinking deeply about things and internalising truth.

Understanding meditation

Read Genesis 24:63. Why is the end of the day a good time to meditate? In what way can worry be seen as a negative form of meditation? What do you think should be the object of a more positive form of meditation?

Read Luke 2:19. Mary had seen and heard many wonderful things, almost too much to take in all at once. How did she retain the benefit of what she had experienced? What do you think is the difference between 'treasured up' and 'pondered'? Note that these are two important activities in meditation.

Read Psalm 1:1–3. If we want to know God's blessing, what should we be careful not to do (v. 1), and what should we be disciplined to practise (v. 2)? How might the first undermine our faith, and how might the second help our faith? What do we see in verse 3 as the benefit of regularly meditating on scripture?

Read Philippians 4:8. How does Paul broaden the legitimate subjects for meditation beyond the word of God? What sort of things might he have had in mind, and what would you include?

Practising meditation together

1   Choose a verse of scripture that seems relevant and helpful to you. Consider the context in which it appears so that you understand it properly. Read it aloud together several times in the same Bible version so that you become familiar with it. Take a moment, if possible, to memorise it.

Then chew the sentence over in your mind, savouring every word and seeking to understand what it is saying. Ask the Holy Spirit to give you wisdom and insight.

For example, take 'Be still and know that I am God' (Psalm 46:10). Consider the following phrases and words:

- I am God
- *Know* that I am God
- Be *still*
- Be still *and* know
- Be still and know that I am God
- *Be*

Next, apply the words to yourself very directly. Make any pronouns personal so that the word is directed to you individually.

Ask yourself, 'What does this verse say to me? How does it affect me? How can I respond to it?'

2 Another way to meditate on scripture is to sing meditatively. This is a style of singing associated with the Taizé Community in France, but also with Gregorian chants. One meditation that I particularly enjoy is 'O Lord, hear my prayer', which can be found on the CD *Taizé Chants* by the St Thomas Music Group (Maragret Rizza), produced by Alliance Music.

3 Do a *lectio divina* study together. Some suitable passages to begin with are Song of Songs 2:14–15; Isaiah 42:1–4; Psalm 63:1–4; Matthew 11:28–30. Follow the guidelines given in Chapter 13 for a group approach.

4 Get hold of a print of Rembrandt's painting *The Return of the Prodigal*, or find a picture on the internet and project it on to a screen so that it is large enough for people to see easily. Perhaps read the story from Luke 15:11–32.

I sometimes play the song 'All I want to do is to bless you' by Marilyn Baker (*Changing Me / Overflow of Worship*, Kingsway Music, KMC CD2388) as people meditate on the picture. The words are suggestive of what the father may be saying to the son.

Share some of the insights from Henri Nouwen's book, *The Return of the Prodigal Son* (DLT, 1994) if you have read it, or Timothy Keller's *The Prodigal God* (Hodder, 2008).

Practising meditation by yourself during the week

Try to read a passage of scripture imaginatively, in the way described in Chapter 15. Here is an example from Mark 10:46–52, the story of blind Bartimaeus. Read the story through a few times to become familiar with it, then seek to enter into it by imagining you are Bartimaeus.

• What do you think it feels like to be blind? To be a beggar? How do people treat you, and how do you feel about their attitude?

- Why are you so insistent that Jesus can help you? What is the significance of your request for mercy?
- How do you feel when you hear that Jesus is calling you? What might you need to lay aside to get closer to him, apart from your cloak?
- When Jesus says, 'What do you want me to do for you?' how do you respond? What kind of 'blindness' in your own life do you want to be removed? What is the deepest desire of your heart?
- What does it mean for you to follow Jesus? Where is he leading you?

Journal any thoughts you may have.

6 Contemplation: the opportunity to receive God's love

In contemplation we become aware of the presence of God and have an assurance that we are loved by him, unconditionally and for all time. It is a God-given moment of connectedness and communion with himself that cannot be forced, only enjoyed when it comes.

Understanding contemplation

Read Psalm 27:4. David, the warrior king, is not afraid to speak about intimacy with God. What is his priority? What do you think it means to 'gaze upon the beauty of the Lord'? How does David intend to go about this?

Read Hebrews 12:1–3. What does it mean to fix our eyes on Jesus? How do we do that, practically? What might we need to let go of? What should we take hold of? What could be the outcome if we take time to consider Jesus?

Read 1 John 4:19. Contemplation has been described as 'an in-loveness felt and experienced'. According to John (the beloved disciple), where does contemplation begin? What is its focus? What effect does dwelling on the love of God have in our lives?

Read 2 Corinthians 3:18 (note that the NIV gives an alternative reading for 'reflect' – 'contemplate'). How does Paul suggest that transformation of character and life takes place? Into what are we being changed? Who is the agent of this change? Is it a crisis or a process?

Practising contemplation together

By its very nature, contemplation cannot be made to happen, and is more normally an individual experience. However, we sometimes find moments in congregational worship when God draws near in a special way and we become aware of his loving presence. At such times, it is important to recognise what is happening and go with the flow of what the Spirit is doing.

1 If this fits within the style of your group, spend some time in 'soaking prayer'. Provide a comfortable venue where people can relax. Play some quiet music and songs that speak of God's love and grace. Invite people to spend some time resting in God's presence, allowing themselves to be loved by him and listening individually to what he wants to say to them. Let people sit, kneel, lie down or walk about as they wish. Spend about 30 minutes in this way. Allow time for people to share anything they have received from God during this time.

2 Spend some time meditating on some of the key verses that speak about God's love for us. Here is a golden thread through scripture that I often follow myself. You may like to mark them in your Bible for future reference. Choose two or three to meditate upon, asking the Holy Spirit to take the truth from your head and reveal it to your heart.

- Jeremiah 31:3
- John 15:9
- Romans 5:8
- Galatians 2:20
- Ephesians 3:17–18
- Ephesians 5:1
- 1 Thessalonians 1:4
- 2 Thessalonians 2:13
- 1 John 4:10, 19
- Jude 1, 21

3 Work slowly through the three stages of contemplation described by Jim Borst and identified in Chapter 14:

- Relaxing: slowing down, becoming still, focusing on God's presence.
- Drawing closer: letting go of hindrances, asking for a fresh touch from God.
- Enjoyment: allowing yourself to be loved, being at rest, moving into prayer.

Practising contemplation by yourself during the week

1 John, the writer of the fourth gospel and some epistles, describes himself as 'the disciple whom Jesus loved' (John 13:23–25; 19:26; 20:2; 21:7, 20). He was the one who sat next to Jesus at the last supper and leaned on his breast, a position of great intimacy.

Such a place is the prerogative of every child of God. In prayer, visualise yourself leaning back on Jesus and resting your head upon his shoulder. You don't need to do or say anything. Simply allow the realisation that you are loved in the way that John was loved. You too are special and his beloved. Let the focus move from you to him.

2 Try a spot of 'Son-bathing'! When we go out into the sunshine, we don't have to make the sun shine on us: it just does. It is the nature of the sun to shine, and to enjoy its warmth requires no effort on our part other than to step out of the shadows and into the light.

Imagine yourself sitting in the sunshine when it is just pleasantly warm, perhaps relaxing in a deckchair. Feel the warmth on your skin, doing you good. Now imagine that the warmth is the Father's love streaming towards you. You don't need to do anything other than receive this love. Allow it to soak into your very being as you know yourself to be loved. When using this exercise, I often listen to tracks 5 and 6 from *Personal Worship* by Stuart Townend (Kingsway Music, KMCD2214).

3 As you begin to be more aware of your own belovedness, begin to share and express God's love in all your relationships. Smile more, be friendly and happy, practise some random acts of kindness, show compassion, share your faith sensitively: the love you receive has to be given away. Contemplation is never an end in itself, only a beginning. We are called to be contemplative activists, so be listening all the time to the way in which God wants his love to flow through you into our needy world.

4 Journal your thoughts at this point.

Notes

1 'You've placed a hunger' by Stuart Townend (Thankyou Music, 1999) Adm. by worshiptogether.com songs excl. UK and Europe, adm. by Kingswaysongs, a division of David C. Cook. tym@kingsway.co.uk. Used by permission.

2 Brent Curtis and John Eldredge, *The Sacred Romance: Drawing closer to the heart of God* (Thomas Nelson, 1997).

3 Curtis and Eldredge, *The Sacred Romance*, p. 7.

4 Tom and Christine Sine, *Living on Purpose: Finding God's best for your life* (Monarch, 2002), p. 8.

5 Sine and Sine, *Living on Purpose*, p. 9.

6 Steve McVey, *A Divine Invitation: Experiencing the romance of God's amazing love* (Harvest House, 2002), p. 140.

7 See David K. Gillett, *Trust and Obey: Explorations in evangelical spirituality* (DLT, 1999), p. 6. This book gives a very helpful overview of the strengths and weaknesses of evangelical spirituality.

8 For a discussion on the identification of particular 'types' of Christian spirituality, see Alister E. McGrath, *Christian Spirituality: An introduction* (Blackwell, 1999), chapter 2. See also Bradley P. Holt, *A Brief History of Christian Spirituality* (Lion Hudson, 1993).

9 For an analysis of the essential characteristics of evangelicalism, see Gillett, *Trust and Obey*, ch. 1, McGrath, *Christian Spirituality*, pp. 18–19, and James M. Gordon, *Evangelical Spirituality* (SPCK, 1991), p. 7. This book looks at evangelicalism through the writings of 22 leading evangelicals from the 18th century to the present day.

10 Gillett, *Trust and Obey*, p. 78.

11 See Dave Tomlinson, *The Post-Evangelical* (Triangle, 1995), p. 15. He gives a penetrating analysis of the state of the evangelical church, although I do not agree with all his conclusions or suggestions for the way forward. In a similar way, Rob McAlpine, *Post Charismatic* (Kingsway, 2006) takes a challenging look at the charismatic movement from within.

12 See Tomlinson, *The Post-Evangelical*, p. 3, and Alan Jamieson, *A Churchless Faith: Faith journeys beyond the churches* (SPCK, 2002)

for an analysis of why many people leave evangelical and charismatic churches.

13 See Tomlinson, *The Post-Evangelical*, p. 10.

14 See Gillett, *Trust and Obey*, ch. 3.

15 Gillett, *Trust and Obey*, p. 159.

16 R.A. Torrey, *How to Succeed in the Christian Life* (Revell, 1906), p. 82.

17 C.H. Spurgeon, *An All Round Ministry* (Banner of Truth, 1960), p. 272.

18 Gordon, *Evangelical Spirituality*, p. 316.

19 Gordon, *Evangelical Spirituality*, p. 328.

20 Pamela Evans, *Driven Beyond the Call of God: Discovering the rhythms of grace* (BRF, 1999), p. 11.

21 Evans, *Driven Beyond the Call of God*, p. 197.

22 Gillett, *Trust and Obey*, p. 177.

23 Gillett, *Trust and Obey*, p. 172.

24 David Ellis, article in *East Asia Millions* (Jan–Mar 1998).

25 David Runcorn, *Space for God: Silence and solitude in the Christian life* (Daybreak, 1990), p. 4.

26 Runcorn, *Space for God*, p. 4.

27 Runcorn, *Space for God*, p. 5.

28 William Barclay, *The Gospel of Mark* (St Andrews Press, 1954), p. 156.

29 Barclay, *Gospel of Mark*, pp. 156–57.

30 Barclay, *Gospel of Mark*, pp. 156–57.

31 A phrase coined by James Gleick in his book *Faster: The acceleration of just about everything* (Vintage, 1999). He describes the ever-increasing pace of life and the effect it has on people as they desperately try to keep up. By and large, the church allows itself to be caught up in the same rush to do more things more quickly. Rather than modelling a different lifestyle, we are carried along on the same tide of ceaseless activity.

32 Rick Warren, *The Purpose-Driven Life* (Zondervan, 2002).

33 Bruce Wilkinson, *Secrets of the Vine: Breaking through to abundance* (Multnomah, 2002), p. 93.

34 Wilkinson, *Secrets of the Vine*, p. 96.

35 Andrew Murray, *Abide in Christ* (Nisbet, 1887), p. 7.

36 McVey, *Divine Invitation*, p. 134.

37 Michael Frye, 'Be the centre' (Vineyard Songs, 1999, UK/Eire) available on the CD *Hungry* (Vineyard Music).

38 Andrew Murray, *The Holiest of All* (Marshall, Morgan and Scott, 1960), p. 484.

39 *Christianity and Renewal* magazine (February 2001).

40 For a fuller discussion of the value of retreats, see John Pearce, *Advance by Retreat: Using silence to come closer to God* (Grove, 1989); Margaret Silf, *Soul Space: Making a retreat in the Christian tradition* (SPCK, 2002). For those in England, The Retreat Association is a helpful starting-point (retreats.org.uk).

41 Wanda Nash, *Christ, Stress and Glory* (DLT, 1997). See the section on pp. 27–32 for a helpful explanation of appropriate breathing, and the difference between 'belly breathing' and 'chest breathing'. See pp. 172–77 for practical guidance on how to be still with God.

42 Simon Barrington-Ward, *The Jesus Prayer* (BRF, 2007).

43 For an explanation and application of the sabbath principle in relation to modern living, see Wayne Muller, *Sabbath Rest: Restoring the sacred rhythm of rest* (Lion, 1999); Marva J. Dawn, *Keeping the Sabbath Wholly: Ceasing, resting, embracing, feasting* (Eerdmans, 1989); Keri Wyatt Kent, *Rest: Living in sabbath simplicity* (Zondervan, 2009).

44 Richard Foster, *Prayer* (Hodder & Stoughton, 1992). The quotation is from page 100, in an excellent and very relevant chapter called 'The prayer of rest'.

45 Murray, *Holiest of All*, p. 152.

46 Murray, *Holiest of All*, p. 146.

47 Watchman Nee, *Sit, Walk, Stand* (Victory Press, 1957), p. 13.

48 Nee, *Sit, Walk, Stand*, p. 14.

49 Nee, *Sit, Walk, Stand*, p. 14.

50 See Roger Foster, *Celebration of Discipline* (Hodder & Stoughton, 1980) for an excellent introduction to the place and value of the spiritual disciplines, particularly solitude.

51 Quoted by Henri Nouwen in *The Way of the Heart* (DLT, 1981), p. 43.

52 Nouwen, *Way of the Heart*, p. 50.

53 Foster, *Celebration of Discipline*, p. 86.

54 See Foster, *Prayer*, p. 166, and the whole chapter on Contemplative Prayer.

55 Alexander Ryrie, *Silent Waiting: The biblical roots of contemplative spirituality* (Canterbury Press, 1999), p. 132.

56 Foster, *Celebration of Discipline*, p. 86.

57 Nouwen, *Way of the Heart*, p. 56.

58 Nouwen, *Way of the Heart*, p. 52.

59 John Main, from an extract in *Spiritual Classics* by Foster and Griffin (Harper Collins, 1999), p. 178.

60 Runcorn, *Space for God*, p. 43.

61 See Nouwen, *Way of the Heart*: 'The Desert Fathers, who lived in the Egyptian Desert during the fourth and fifth centuries, can offer us a very important perspective on our life as ministers living at the end of the twentieth century' (p. 13).

62 From *When Lonely: A book of private prayer*, quoted in Paul Iles, *Touching the Far Corner* (Bible Society, 1996).

63 Nouwen, *Way of the Heart*, p. 27.

64 Runcorn, *Space for God*, p. 23.

65 Foster, *Celebration of Discipline*, p. 2.

66 The 'dark night of the soul' is a metaphor used to describe a phase in a person's spiritual journey marked by a sense of loneliness and abandonment. See *The Collected Works of St John of the Cross* (ICS Publications, 1991).

67 Nouwen, *Way of the Heart*, p. 37.

68 Joyce Huggett, *Open to God* (Hodder & Stoughton, 1989).

69 Ruth Hayley Barton, *Sacred Rhythms: Arranging our lives for spiritual transformation* (IVP, 2006).

70 John Stott, *Guard the Gospel* (IVP, 1973), p. 60.

71 Ken Gire, *The Reflective Life: Becoming more spiritually sensitive to the everyday moments of life* (Kingsway, 1998), p. 11.

72 Gire, *Reflective Life*, p. 25.

73 Gire, *Reflective Life*, pp. 92–93.

74 Richard Peace, *Spiritual Journalling: Recording your journey toward God* (NavPress, 1998), p. 10.

75 Peace, *Spiritual Journalling*, pp. 64–67, has some helpful comments on how we can learn from our dreams.

76 Peace, *Spiritual Journalling*, p. 7.

77 Ryrie, *Silent Waiting*, p. 129. See also his fuller discussion on meditation: pp. 13–17, 125–30.

78 Joyce Huggett, *Learning the Language of Prayer* (BRF, 1994), p. 38.

79 Peter Toon, *Meditating as a Christian: Waiting upon God* (HarperCollins, 1991), p. 59.

80 Toon, *Meditating as a Christian*, p. 62.

81 Foster, *Celebration of Discipline*, p. 22.

82 Alister McGrath, *The Journey: A pilgrim in the lands of the Spirit* (Hodder & Stoughton, 1999), pp. 16, 17.

83 Margaret Magdalen, *Jesus Man of Prayer* (Eagle, 1987), p. 23.

84 Henri Nouwen, *The Return of the Prodigal Son* (DLT, 1994).

85 Thomas Merton, *Spiritual Direction and Meditation* (Liturgical Press, 1998), quoted by Foster in *Prayer*, p. 162.

86 Norvene Vest, *Knowing By Heart: Bible reading for spiritual growth* (DLT, 1995), p. 3.
87 Richard Peace, *Contemplative Bible Reading* (NavPress, 1998), pp. 12–13.
88 Vest, *Knowing By Heart*, pp. 4–5.
89 Huggett, *Learning the Language of Prayer*, p. 42.
90 Ryrie, *Silent Waiting*, p. 4.
91 Ryrie, *Silent Waiting*, p. 164.
92 Ryrie, *Silent Waiting*, p. 165.
93 Stephen Verney, *Into the New Age* (Fontana, 1976), p. 91.
94 Jim Borst, *Coming to God in the Stillness* (Eagle, 1992).
95 Simon Holt, 'Finding God in the ordinary, the mundane, and the immediate', *Fuller Magazine* (March 1999), p. 23.
96 Brother Lawrence, quoted by Joyce Huggett, *Finding God in the Fast Lane* (Eagle, 1993), p. 28.
97 Timothy Jones, *Awake My Soul: Practical spirituality for busy people* (Doubleday, 1999), p. 3.
98 Jane Eliza Leeson (1807–82).
99 Jones, *Awake My Soul*, p. 70.
100 David Kundtz, *Stopping: How to be still when you have to keep going* (Newleaf, 1998).

Further reading

Here are some more helpful books, not mentioned in the text.

Stillness, silence and solitude
Listening to God, Joyce Huggett (Hodder & Soughton, 2005)
Solitude and Silence, Jan Johnson (IVP, 2003)
The Too Busy Book, Linda Andersen (Waterbrook, 2004)
In Praise of Slow, Karl Honore (Orion, 2004)
Finding Sanctuary, Christopher Jamieson (Orion, 2006)
Do Nothing to Change Your Life, Stephen Cottrell (Church House, 2007)
Working from a Place of Rest, Tony Horsfall (BRF, 2010)
Invitation to Silence and Solitude, Ruth Haley Barton (IVP, 2010)
A Simplified Life, Verena Schiller (Canterbury, 2010)

Reflection
Landmarks, Margaret Silf (DLT, 1998)
Silence on Fire, William Shannon (Crossroad, 2000)
How to Keep a Spiritual Journal, Ron Klug (Augsburg, 2002)
Journal Keeping, Luann Budd (IVP, 2002)
God Is Closer Than You Think, John Ortberg (Zondervan, 2005)
The Attentive Life, Leighton Ford (IVP, 2008)

Bible meditation
Biblical Meditation, Elmer Towns (Regal, 1998)
Listening to God, Jan Johnson (NavPress, 1998)
The Lost Art of Meditation, Sheila Pritchard (SU, 2003)
Savouring God's Word, Jan Johnson (NavPress, 2004)
Into God's Presence, Liz Babbs (Zondervan, 2005)
Eat This Book, Eugene Peterson (Hodder, 2006)
Simple Ways, Gunilla Norris (Blueridge, 2008)
Life with God, Richard Foster (Hodder, 2008)
Meditating with Scripture, Elena Bosetti (BRF, 2010)
The Circle of Love, Ann Persson (BRF, 2010)
Opening to God, David Benner (IVP, 2010)

Contemplation
Simple Prayer, John Dalrymple (DLT, 1984)
Contemplating the Word, Peter Dodson (SPCK, 1987)
The Soul at Rest, Tricia McCary Rhodes (Bethany House, 1996)
Everything Belongs, Richard Rohr (Crossroad, 1999)
When the Soul Listens, Jan Johnson (NavPress, 1999)
Meditation and Contemplation, Timothy Gallagher (Crossroad, 2008)
Pilgrimage of a Soul, Phileena Heuertz (IVP, 2010)

The spiritual disciplines in everyday life
The Spirit of the Disciplines, Dallas Willard (Hodder, 1996)
Enjoying the Presence of God, Jan Johnson (NavPress, 1996)
The Life You've Always Wanted, John Ortberg (Zondervan, 1997)
The Joy of Spiritual Fitness, Ray Simpson (Zondervan, 2003)
Companions of Christ, Margaret Silf (Eerdmans, 2004)
The Sacred Way, Tony Evans (Zondervan, 2005)
Spiritual Disciplines Handbook, Adele Culhoun (IVP, 2005)
Soul Feast, Marjorie Thompson (John Knox, 2005)
A Fruitful Life, Tony Horsfall (BRF, 2006)
Spirituality Workbook, David Runcorn (SPCK, 2006)
Sacred Chaos, Tricia McCary Rhodes (IVP, 2008)
Creative Ideas for Quiet Days, Sue Pickering (Canterbury, 2008)
Creative Retreat Ideas, Sue Pickering (Canterbury, 2008)

Internet sites
Contemplative Outreach UK: couk.org.uk
Fellowship of Contemplative Prayer: contemplative-prayer.org.uk
London Centre for Spiritual Development: lcsd.org.uk
Daily prayer for MP3: pray-as-you-go.org
Rejesus: rejesus.co.uk
The Transforming Center (Ruth Hayley Barton): transformingcenter.org
Renovaré (Richard Foster): renovare.org
Daily prayer and reflection: cradleofprayer.org
Soul Spark (Exploring Spirituality): soulspark.org.uk

Twitter
twitter.com/prayerbullets
twitter.com/MyParable
twitter.com/churchofengland
twitter.com/Virtual_Abbey